Houghton Mifflin Harcourt

Texas
GoMath!
Grade 3

Assessment Guide

- **Prerequisite Skills Inventory**
- **Beginning-of-Year, Middle-of-Year, and End-of-Year Benchmark Tests**
- **Module Tests in TEXAS Assessment Format**
- **Individual Record Forms**
- **Correlations to Texas Essential Knowledge and Skills for Mathematics**

ISBN 978-0-544-06035-7

7 8 9 10 0982 22 21 20 19 18

4500707264   B C D E F G

Contents

Tests and Record Forms

Overview of *Texas GO Math!* Assessment

How Assessment Can Help Individualize Instruction

The *Assessment Guide* contains several types of assessment for use throughout the school year. The following pages will explain how these assessments can help teachers evaluate students' understanding of the Texas Essential Knowledge and Skills (TEKS). This *Assessment Guide* also contains Individual Record Forms (IRF) to help guide teachers' instructional choices to improve students' performance. The record forms may be used to monitor students' progress toward their mastery of the Texas Essential Knowledge and Skills for this grade.

Diagnostic Assessment

Prerequisite Skills Inventory in the *Assessment Guide* should be given at the beginning of the school year or when a new student arrives. This short answer test assesses students' understanding of prerequisite skills. Test results provide information about the review or intervention that students may need in order to be successful in learning the mathematics related to the TEKS for the grade level. The IRF for the Prerequisite Skills Inventory provides suggestions for intervention based on the student's performance.

Beginning-of-Year Test in the *Assessment Guide* should be given early in the year to determine which skills for the current grade students may already understand. The items on this test are in TEXAS assessment format, with multiple-choice and griddable items. This benchmark test will facilitate customization of instructional content to optimize the time spent teaching specific objectives. The IRF for the Beginning-of-Year Test provides suggestions for the intervention based on the student's performance.

Show What You Know in the *Student Edition* is provided for each unit. It assesses prior knowledge from previous grades as well as content taught earlier in the current grade. Teachers can customize instructional content using the suggested intervention options. The assessment should be scheduled at the beginning of each unit to determine if students have the prerequisite skills for the unit.

Formative Assessment

Are You Ready? items appear in the *Assessment Guide*. These are quick checks to determine if students have the prerequisite skills they need for a particular lesson in the *Texas GO Math! Student Edition*. They may be reproduced for each student or shown to the class on a document camera. If several students have trouble with the Are You Ready? items, teachers may wish to review concepts before teaching the next lesson.

Middle-of-Year Test in the *Assessment Guide* assesses the same TEKS as the Beginning-of-Year Test, allowing students' progress to be tracked and providing opportunity for instructional adjustments, when required. The items on this test are in TEXAS assessment format, with multiple-choice and griddable items.

Summative Assessment

Module and Unit Assessments in the *Texas GO Math! Student Edition* indicate whether additional instruction or practice is necessary for students to master the concepts and skills taught in the module or unit. These tests include constructed-response, multiple-choice, and griddable items.

Module and Unit Tests in the *Assessment Guide* evaluate students' mastery of concepts and skills taught in the module or unit. There is a test for each module. When only one module comprises a unit, the unit test assesses the content in just that module. When there are multiple modules in a unit, there are designated module tests and a comprehensive unit test. The items on this test are in TEXAS assessment format, with multiple-choice and griddable items.

End-of-Year Test in the *Assessment Guide* assesses the same TEKS as the Beginning- and Middle-of-Year Tests. The items on this test are in TEXAS assessment format, with multiple-choice and griddable items. It is the final benchmark test for the grade level. When student performance on the End-of-Year Test is compared to performance on Beginning- and Middle-of-Year Tests, teachers are able to document student growth.

Using Correlations to TEKS

The final section of the *Assessment Guide* contains correlations to the TEKS. To identify which items in the *Assessment Guide* test a particular TEKS, locate that TEKS in the chart. The column to the right will list the test and specific items that assess the TEKS. Correlations to TEKS are also provided in the Individual Record Form for each test.

Assessment Technology

Online Assessment System offers flexibility to individualize assessment for each child. Teachers can assign entire tests from the *Assessment Guide* or build customized tests from a bank of items. For customized tests, specific TEKS can be selected to test.

Multiple-choice and fill-in-the-blank items are automatically scored by the Online Assessment System. This provides immediate feedback. Tests may also be printed and administered as paper-and-pencil tests.

The same intervention resources are available in the Online Assessment System as in the *Assessment Guide*. So, whether students take tests online or printed from the Online Assessment System, teachers have access to materials to help students succeed in *Texas GO Math!*

Data-Driven Decision Making

Texas GO Math! allows for quick and accurate data-driven decision making so teachers will have more instructional time to meet students' needs. There are several intervention and review resources available with *Texas GO Math!* Every lesson in the *Student Edition* has a corresponding lesson in the *Texas GO Math! Response to Intervention Tier 1 Lessons* online resource. There are also *Tier 2 Skills* and *Tier 3 Examples* available for students who need further instruction or practice. For online intervention lessons, students may complete lessons in *Soar to Success Math*. These resources provide the foundation for individual prescriptions for students who need extra support.

Using Individual Record Forms

The *Assessment Guide* includes Individual Record Forms (IRF) for all tests. On these forms, each test item is correlated to the TEKS it assesses. There are intervention resources correlated to each item as well. A common error explains why a student may have missed the item. These forms can be used to:

- Follow progress throughout the year.
- Identify strengths and weaknesses.
- Make assignments based on the intervention options provided.

How to Complete a Grid

You will answer some of the problems on the tests for your *Texas GO Math!* book by filling in a grid. This page will explain how to fill in the grid.

You will use a grid like the one at the right to record your answers after you solve problems. The boxes at the top are the answer boxes. The circles with numbers inside them are the answer bubbles.

The directions on the test will say:

> Record your answer and fill in the bubbles on the grid. Be sure to use the correct place value.

Step 1

Read the problem and solve it.

> Tom has 43 crayons in his desk. He has 28 more crayons at home. How many crayons does Tom have altogether?

Step 2

Tom has 71 crayons. Record your answer in the answer boxes. So, write 71.

Step 3

Fill in the bubbles on the grid. To show 71, fill in ⑦ in the tens place and ① in the ones place.

Remember to check the place value of the digits. For example, a one-digit answer must be recorded in the ones place. You may record 0 in the tens and hundreds places or leave them blank.

Answer Sheet for _____ Test

1. Ⓐ Ⓑ Ⓒ Ⓓ
2. Ⓐ Ⓑ Ⓒ Ⓓ
3. Ⓐ Ⓑ Ⓒ Ⓓ
4. Ⓐ Ⓑ Ⓒ Ⓓ
5. Ⓐ Ⓑ Ⓒ Ⓓ

6. Ⓐ Ⓑ Ⓒ Ⓓ
7. Ⓐ Ⓑ Ⓒ Ⓓ
8. Ⓐ Ⓑ Ⓒ Ⓓ
9. Ⓐ Ⓑ Ⓒ Ⓓ
10. Ⓐ Ⓑ Ⓒ Ⓓ

11. Ⓐ Ⓑ Ⓒ Ⓓ
12. Ⓐ Ⓑ Ⓒ Ⓓ
13. Ⓐ Ⓑ Ⓒ Ⓓ
14. Ⓐ Ⓑ Ⓒ Ⓓ
15. Ⓐ Ⓑ Ⓒ Ⓓ

16. Ⓐ Ⓑ Ⓒ Ⓓ
17. Ⓐ Ⓑ Ⓒ Ⓓ
18. Ⓐ Ⓑ Ⓒ Ⓓ
19. Ⓐ Ⓑ Ⓒ Ⓓ
20. Ⓐ Ⓑ Ⓒ Ⓓ

21. Ⓐ Ⓑ Ⓒ Ⓓ
22. Ⓐ Ⓑ Ⓒ Ⓓ
23. Ⓐ Ⓑ Ⓒ Ⓓ
24. Ⓐ Ⓑ Ⓒ Ⓓ
25. Ⓐ Ⓑ Ⓒ Ⓓ

26. Ⓐ Ⓑ Ⓒ Ⓓ
27. Ⓐ Ⓑ Ⓒ Ⓓ
28. Ⓐ Ⓑ Ⓒ Ⓓ
29. Ⓐ Ⓑ Ⓒ Ⓓ
30. Ⓐ Ⓑ Ⓒ Ⓓ

31. Ⓐ Ⓑ Ⓒ Ⓓ
32. Ⓐ Ⓑ Ⓒ Ⓓ
33. Ⓐ Ⓑ Ⓒ Ⓓ
34. Ⓐ Ⓑ Ⓒ Ⓓ
35. Ⓐ Ⓑ Ⓒ Ⓓ

36. Ⓐ Ⓑ Ⓒ Ⓓ
37. Ⓐ Ⓑ Ⓒ Ⓓ
38. Ⓐ Ⓑ Ⓒ Ⓓ
39. Ⓐ Ⓑ Ⓒ Ⓓ
40. Ⓐ Ⓑ Ⓒ Ⓓ

41. Ⓐ Ⓑ Ⓒ Ⓓ
42. Ⓐ Ⓑ Ⓒ Ⓓ
43. Ⓐ Ⓑ Ⓒ Ⓓ
44. Ⓐ Ⓑ Ⓒ Ⓓ
45. Ⓐ Ⓑ Ⓒ Ⓓ

46. Ⓐ Ⓑ Ⓒ Ⓓ
47. Ⓐ Ⓑ Ⓒ Ⓓ
48. Ⓐ Ⓑ Ⓒ Ⓓ
49. Ⓐ Ⓑ Ⓒ Ⓓ
50. Ⓐ Ⓑ Ⓒ Ⓓ

Grids for _____ Test

Number _____

			.
⓪	⓪	⓪	
①	①	①	
②	②	②	
③	③	③	
④	④	④	
⑤	⑤	⑤	
⑥	⑥	⑥	
⑦	⑦	⑦	
⑧	⑧	⑧	
⑨	⑨	⑨	

Number _____

			.
⓪	⓪	⓪	
①	①	①	
②	②	②	
③	③	③	
④	④	④	
⑤	⑤	⑤	
⑥	⑥	⑥	
⑦	⑦	⑦	
⑧	⑧	⑧	
⑨	⑨	⑨	

Number _____

			.
⓪	⓪	⓪	
①	①	①	
②	②	②	
③	③	③	
④	④	④	
⑤	⑤	⑤	
⑥	⑥	⑥	
⑦	⑦	⑦	
⑧	⑧	⑧	
⑨	⑨	⑨	

Number _____

			.
⓪	⓪	⓪	
①	①	①	
②	②	②	
③	③	③	
④	④	④	
⑤	⑤	⑤	
⑥	⑥	⑥	
⑦	⑦	⑦	
⑧	⑧	⑧	
⑨	⑨	⑨	

Number _____

		.	.
⓪	⓪	⓪	
①	①	①	
②	②	②	
③	③	③	
④	④	④	
⑤	⑤	⑤	
⑥	⑥	⑥	
⑦	⑦	⑦	
⑧	⑧	⑧	
⑨	⑨	⑨	

Number _____

			.
⓪	⓪	⓪	
①	①	①	
②	②	②	
③	③	③	
④	④	④	
⑤	⑤	⑤	
⑥	⑥	⑥	
⑦	⑦	⑦	
⑧	⑧	⑧	
⑨	⑨	⑨	

1. Which of these is a way to model the number 146?

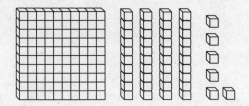

Ⓐ 1 hundred 46 tens

Ⓑ 14 hundreds 6 ones

Ⓒ 14 tens 6 ones

Ⓓ 146 tens

2. Which of the following numbers has 7 tens, 5 ones, and 3 hundreds?

Ⓐ 753

Ⓑ 375

Ⓒ 357

Ⓓ 537

1. Which is NOT a way to model the number 2,804 with base-ten blocks?

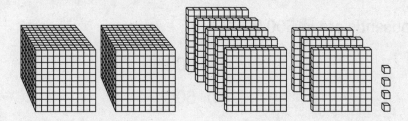

Ⓐ 2 thousands 804 tens

Ⓑ 1 thousand 18 hundreds 4 ones

Ⓒ 28 hundreds 4 ones

Ⓓ 2 thousands 8 hundreds 4 ones

2. Which shows the number 7,205 in expanded form?

Ⓐ 7,000 + 200 + 50

Ⓑ 7 + 2 + 0 + 5

Ⓒ 7,000 + 200 + 5

Ⓓ 70 + 20 + 5

Name _____

1. What is the value of the digit 8 in the number 78,462?

    Ⓐ 80,000

    Ⓑ 80

    Ⓒ 800

    Ⓓ 8,000

2. In the number 31,590, what digit is in the ten thousands place?

    Ⓐ 9

    Ⓑ 1

    Ⓒ 5

    Ⓓ 3

Name _____

1. How many thousands are in 500,000?

    Ⓐ 5   Ⓒ 500

    Ⓑ 5,000   Ⓓ 50

2. Unscramble the place values. Write the number in standard form.

    6 tens + 2 ten thousands + 8 ones + 9 thousands + 4 hundred thousands + 3 hundreds

    Ⓐ 628,943   Ⓒ 349,826

    Ⓑ 234,689   Ⓓ 429,368

1. Which of the following is true?

Ⓐ 852 > 825

Ⓒ 352 > 567

Ⓑ 471 = 319

Ⓓ 1,000 < 898

---

2. Write the numbers 2,530; 826; 1,947; and 2,035 in order from least to greatest.

Ⓐ 2,530; 826; 1,947; 2,035

Ⓒ 826; 1,947; 2,530; 2,035

Ⓑ 826; 1,947; 2,035; 2,530

Ⓓ 2,530; 2,035; 1,947; 826

Name _____

1. A piece of ribbon is cut into thirds. How many pieces of ribbon are there?

(A) 6

(B) 3

(C) 2

(D) 4

2. Which shape has parts that are fourths?

(A)

(B)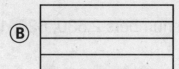

(C)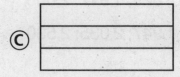

(D)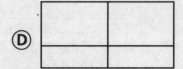

Name _____

1. How many equal parts are in the whole?

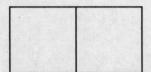

(A) 6 equal parts

(B) 4 equal parts

(C) 2 equal parts

(D) 3 equal parts

2. Which shape has three equal parts?

(A) 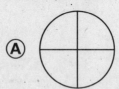   (B)

(C) 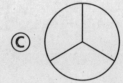   (D)

1. How many equal parts are in the whole?

(A) 4

(B) 6

(C) 2

(D) 8

2. What fraction names the shaded part of the whole?

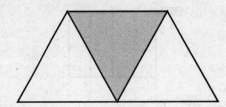

(A) $\frac{1}{6}$

(B) $\frac{1}{3}$

(C) $\frac{1}{4}$

(D) $\frac{1}{2}$

1. Which fraction names each part of the whole?

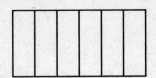

(A) $\frac{1}{2}$

(B) $\frac{1}{6}$

(C) $\frac{1}{4}$

(D) $\frac{1}{3}$

2. What fraction is shown by the point?

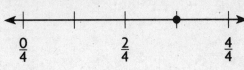

(A) $\frac{3}{5}$

(B) $\frac{4}{3}$

(C) $\frac{1}{4}$

(D) $\frac{3}{4}$

1. Which fraction names each
part of the whole?

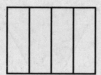

  Ⓐ $\frac{1}{4}$

  Ⓑ $\frac{1}{6}$

  Ⓒ $\frac{1}{3}$

  Ⓓ $\frac{1}{2}$

2. What fraction names the shaded
part of the whole?

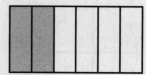

  Ⓐ $\frac{4}{6}$

  Ⓑ $\frac{2}{8}$

  Ⓒ $\frac{2}{6}$

  Ⓓ $\frac{3}{6}$

Name _____

1. Which numerator makes the statement true?

$$\frac{3}{8} > \frac{\blacksquare}{8}$$

1

| $\frac{1}{8}$ | $\frac{1}{8}$ | $\frac{1}{8}$ |

- (A) 7
- (B) 5
- (C) 6
- (D) 1

2. Which symbol makes the statement true?

$$\frac{4}{6} \,\bullet\, \frac{2}{6}$$

- (A) =
- (B) >
- (C) <
- (D) none

Name _____

1. Which correctly compares the fractions?

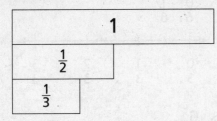

1

| $\frac{1}{2}$ |

| $\frac{1}{3}$ |

- (A) $\frac{1}{2} = \frac{1}{2}$
- (B) $\frac{1}{2} > \frac{1}{3}$
- (C) $\frac{1}{2} < 1.3$
- (D) $\frac{1}{3} > \frac{1}{2}$

2. Which fraction is greater than $\frac{1}{3}$?

- (A) $\frac{1}{2}$
- (B) $\frac{1}{4}$
- (C) $\frac{1}{6}$
- (D) $\frac{1}{8}$

Name _____

1. Which comparison statement is correct?

Ⓐ $\frac{3}{4} < \frac{7}{8}$

Ⓑ $\frac{3}{8} = \frac{5}{8}$

Ⓒ $\frac{1}{2} > \frac{2}{3}$

Ⓓ $\frac{4}{6} < \frac{4}{8}$

2. Which symbol makes the statement true?

$$\frac{5}{6} \ \bullet \ \frac{5}{8}$$

Ⓐ =

Ⓑ >

Ⓒ <

Ⓓ none

Name _____

1. Which fraction is equivalent to $\frac{2}{4}$?

1	
$\frac{1}{4}$	$\frac{1}{4}$

Ⓐ $\frac{1}{3}$

Ⓑ $\frac{1}{8}$

Ⓒ $\frac{1}{2}$

Ⓓ $\frac{1}{6}$

2. Which fraction is equivalent to $\frac{2}{3}$?

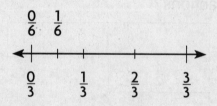

Ⓐ $\frac{6}{6}$

Ⓑ $\frac{3}{6}$

Ⓒ $\frac{2}{6}$

Ⓓ $\frac{4}{6}$

1. Which fraction is equivalent to $\frac{3}{3}$?

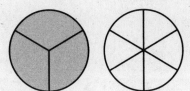

Ⓐ $\frac{6}{3}$

Ⓑ $\frac{2}{3}$

Ⓒ $\frac{3}{6}$

Ⓓ $\frac{6}{6}$

2. Which fraction is equivalent to $\frac{6}{8}$?

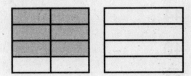

Ⓐ $\frac{1}{4}$

Ⓑ $\frac{2}{8}$

Ⓒ $\frac{3}{4}$

Ⓓ $\frac{1}{2}$

1. Which number is closest to 50?

Ⓐ 44

Ⓑ 40

Ⓒ 38

Ⓓ 48

---

2. Which number is closest to 200?

Ⓐ 252

Ⓑ 205

Ⓒ 236

Ⓓ 220

1. What is the nearest ten to 34?

Ⓐ 26   Ⓑ 40

Ⓒ 30   Ⓓ 50

---

2. What is the nearest hundred to 170?

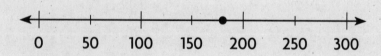

Ⓐ 200   Ⓑ 170

Ⓒ 190   Ⓓ 100

1. Find 46 + 13.

(A) 69

(B) 59

(C) 33

(D) 49

2. Find 53 + 29.

(A) 82

(B) 712

(C) 72

(D) 80

1. Which is the expanded form of 702?

(A) 700 + 2

(B) 700 + 100 + 2

(C) seven hundred two

(D) 7,000 + 100 + 20

2. What is 346 rounded to the nearest ten?

(A) 400

(B) 300

(C) 350

(D) 340

Name _____

1. What is the sum of 35 and 15?

   Ⓐ 60

   Ⓑ 770

   Ⓒ 50

   Ⓓ 40

2. What is the estimated sum of 572 and 124 to the nearest hundred?

   Ⓐ 700

   Ⓑ 570

   Ⓒ 690

   Ⓓ 600

Name _____

1. What is the total value of these coins?

   Ⓐ 75¢   Ⓑ 40¢

   Ⓒ 60¢   Ⓓ 25¢

2. What is the total value of these bills?

   Ⓐ $7.00   Ⓑ $2.00

   Ⓒ $15.00   Ⓓ $5.00

1. Which number has the underlined digit in the tens place?

   Ⓐ 5̲22

   Ⓑ 375̲

   Ⓒ 87̲0

   Ⓓ 142̲

2. Round 276 to the nearest hundreds place.

   Ⓐ 100

   Ⓑ 280

   Ⓒ 300

   Ⓓ 200

1. Find the difference.

   55 − 12

   Ⓐ 60   Ⓒ 43

   Ⓑ 67   Ⓓ 70

2. Find the difference.   77
                          − 14

   Ⓐ 63   Ⓒ 60

   Ⓑ 91   Ⓓ 51

Name _____

1. Find the difference.   72
                            − 24

   Ⓐ 48

   Ⓑ 94

   Ⓒ 56

   Ⓓ 46

---

2. Find the difference.   51
                            − 38

   Ⓐ 89   Ⓒ 13

   Ⓑ 27   Ⓓ 23

- -

Name _____

1. Find the difference.

60 − 13

   Ⓐ 47

   Ⓑ 73

   Ⓒ 53

   Ⓓ 57

2. Find the difference.   91
                            − 37

   Ⓐ 128

   Ⓑ 91

   Ⓒ 54

   Ⓓ 64

Name _____

1. What is the sum?

$2 + 2 + 2$

Ⓐ 8

Ⓑ 2

Ⓒ 6

Ⓓ 5

2. Which tells how many in all?

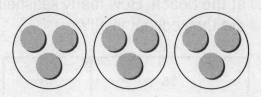

Ⓐ 6

Ⓑ 9

Ⓒ 3

Ⓓ 12

Name _____

1. What are the next two numbers if you skip count by 2?

2, 4, 6, ____, ____

Ⓐ 7, 8

Ⓑ 8, 10

Ⓒ 10, 12

Ⓓ 8, 9

2. What is the sum?

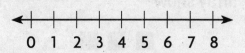

$2 + 5$

Ⓐ 7

Ⓑ 8

Ⓒ 6

Ⓓ 5

Name _____

1. Ava and Luke collected seashells at the beach. How many seashells did they collect in all?

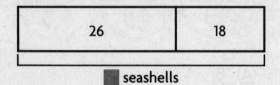

seashells

(A) 34

(B) 8

(C) 40

(D) 44

2. Lily made necklaces for her friends. She used 45 green beads and 76 red beads. How many beads did Lily use in all?

(A) 31

(B) 121

(C) 111

(D) 91

Name _____

1. What addition sentence does the array show?

(A) 2 + 2 = 4

(B) 2 + 3 = 5

(C) 3 + 3 = 6

(D) 4 + 4 = 8

2. Jose made 3 groups of 8 marbles. How many marbles did he use?

(A) 21

(B) 16

(C) 24

(D) 11

1. What multiplication sentence does the array show?

Ⓐ 3 × 4 = 12

Ⓑ 3 × 3 = 9

Ⓒ 3 × 2 = 6

Ⓓ 4 × 4 = 16

2. Which is an example of the Commutative Property of Addition?

Ⓐ 3 + 4 = 4 + 3

Ⓑ 4 + 2 = 3 + 2

Ⓒ 1 + 3 = 1 + 3

Ⓓ 5 + 2 = 2 × 5

1. A model car costs $3. What is the price of 4 model cars?

Ⓐ $20

Ⓑ $12

Ⓒ $7

Ⓓ $14

2. Nita has 5 model cars. Each model car has 4 wheels. How many wheels do the model cars have in all?

Ⓐ 15

Ⓑ 1

Ⓒ 9

Ⓓ 20

1. What equal groups does the model show?

   Ⓐ 2 groups of 2

   Ⓑ 4 groups of 4

   Ⓒ 4 groups of 2

   Ⓓ 2 groups of 4

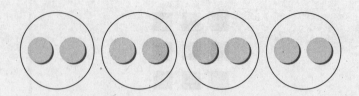

2. Which is the doubles fact for the model?

   Ⓐ 4 + 4 = 8

   Ⓑ 2 + 2 = 4

   Ⓒ 1 + 4 = 5

   Ⓓ 8 + 2 = 10

1. Which number will come next?

   10, 20, 30, 40, __?__

   Ⓐ 41

   Ⓑ 55

   Ⓒ 30

   Ⓓ 50

2. What equal groups does the model show?

   Ⓐ 5 groups of 3

   Ⓑ 3 groups of 3

   Ⓒ 3 groups of 5

   Ⓓ 5 groups of 5

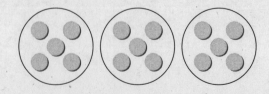

1. What equal groups does the model show?

   Ⓐ 6 groups of 3

   Ⓑ 6 groups of 6

   Ⓒ 3 groups of 6

   Ⓓ 3 groups of 3

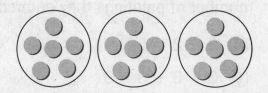

2. Which fact does the model show?

   Ⓐ $2 \times 2 = 4$

   Ⓑ $4 \times 2 = 8$

   Ⓒ $4 + 4 = 8$

   Ⓓ $2 \times 4 = 8$

1. Which multiplication sentence does the array show?

   Ⓐ $2 \times 4 = 8$

   Ⓑ $3 + 4 = 7$

   Ⓒ $3 \times 4 = 12$

   Ⓓ $6 \times 2 = 12$

2. What is the product of 4×6?

   Ⓐ 10

   Ⓑ 12

   Ⓒ 8

   Ⓓ 24

1. Addison, Jacob, and Olivia each entered two paintings in the school art show. Which number sentence shows the total number of paintings they entered?

   (A) $3 + 2 = 5$

   (B) $3 + 3 + 3 = 9$

   (C) $3 \times 2 = 6$

   (D) $3 \times 3 = 9$

2. Christopher and Sophia each sold 10 tickets to the class play. Which shows the total number of tickets they sold?

   (A) $2 \times 10 = 20$

   (B) $2 + 2 = 4$

   (C) $2 + 10 = 12$

   (D) $10 - 2 = 8$

1. Ava's dog had seven puppies. How many ears do seven puppies have?

   (A) 7

   (B) 9

   (C) 2

   (D) 14

2. Caleb and his family spent two weeks camping at Yellowstone National Park. How many days was Caleb's family camping?

   (A) 7

   (B) 14

   (C) 9

   (D) 5

1. Connor has bags of marbles. Each bag has 8 marbles. He gives 4 bags of marbles to each of 2 friends. How many marbles did Connor give away?

   (A) 64

   (B) 14

   (C) 32

   (D) 8

2. Which number sentence is an example of the Associative Property of Multiplication?

   (A) $7 + 8 = 8 + 7$

   (B) $5 \times 6 = 6 \times 5$

   (C) $(6 \times 5) \times 2 = 6 \times (5 \times 2)$

   (D) $(9 + 3) + 4 = 9 + (3 + 4)$

1. Which of the following describes this pattern:

   7, 14, 21, 28, 35

   (A) Multiply by 7

   (B) Add 7

   (C) Multiply by 8

   (D) Subtract 7

2. When Hannah finds the multiplication facts for 4, which digit will NOT be in the ones place of the product?

   (A) 3

   (B) 2

   (C) 8

   (D) 4

1. Cameron is putting tiles on a patio floor. He will lay 8 rows of tiles with 6 tiles in each row. How many tiles will Cameron use?

Ⓐ 14   Ⓒ 56

Ⓑ 42   Ⓓ 48

2. Emily bought 5 bags of apples at the farmers' market. How many apples did she buy?

Ⓐ 40

Ⓑ 13

Ⓒ 32

Ⓓ 48

Bags	1	2	3	4	5
Apples	8	16	24	▇	▇

1. The students in the band stood in 4 rows of 9 students for the school yearbook picture. How many students were in the photo?

Ⓐ 13   Ⓒ 36

Ⓑ 27   Ⓓ 5

2. How many wheels are on 9 tricycles and 4 bicycles?

Ⓐ 13

Ⓑ 35

Ⓒ 27

Ⓓ 8

1. Jacob's mother bought 6 boxes of energy bars for soccer practice. Each box had 10 bars. How many energy bars did she buy?

Ⓐ 16

Ⓑ 4

Ⓒ 60

Ⓓ 50

2. There are 3 after-school clubs. Each club has 20 students. How many students are in the after-school clubs?

Ⓐ 60

Ⓑ 23

Ⓒ 30

Ⓓ 17

1. Alexis represented the number of rolls of dimes she has and the number of dimes in each roll on a number line. How many dimes does she have?

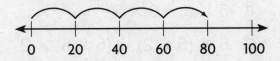

Ⓐ 10

Ⓑ 40

Ⓒ 20

Ⓓ 80

2. Josh represented the number of pairs of skates the skating rink rents in a week and the number of weeks in 2 months on a number line. How many pairs of skates did the skating rink rent?

Ⓐ 100

Ⓑ 500

Ⓒ 400

Ⓓ 450

Name _____

1. What is the missing number?

3 tens 12 ones = ▩ tens 2 ones

(A) 2   (C) 1

(B) 4   (D) 3

---

2. What is the missing number?

25 tens = ▩ hundreds 5 tens

(A) 2   (C) 3

(B) 5   (D) 1

Name _____

1. Madison has a collection of stickers. There are 14 stickers in each of 6 envelopes. How can she model on grid paper the number of stickers she has?

(A) 4 rows of 8 and 2 rows of 6

(B) 6 rows of 6 and 6 rows of 6

(C) 6 rows of 10 and 6 rows of 4

(D) 6 rows of 10 and 4 rows of 4

2. Which number sentence is an example of the Distributive Property of Multiplication?

(A) $7 \times 0 = 0$

(B) $5 \times 6 = 6 \times 5$

(C) $6 \times (5 \times 2) = (6 \times 5) \times 2$

(D) $9 \times 30 = 9 \times (10 + 10 + 10)$

1. Paulo plays lacrosse for a club. The trip from his house to the practice field is 20 miles round-trip. If he practices 5 days a week, how far does he travel in one week?

   Ⓐ 25

   Ⓑ 100

   Ⓒ 150

   Ⓓ 200

2. What are the partial products when you multiply 6×53?

   Ⓐ 18 and 300

   Ⓑ 18 and 30

   Ⓒ 180 and 30

   Ⓓ 300 and 180

Name _____

1. How many counters are in each group?

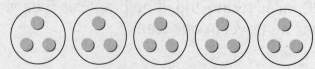

(A) 10   (C) 3

(B) 2   (D) 5

---

2. Which tells how many in all?

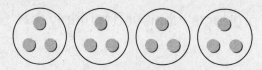

(A) 4   (C) 3

(B) 12   (D) 9

- -

Name _____

1. How many groups are shown?

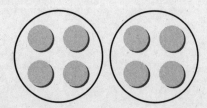

(A) 6

(B) 4

(C) 2

(D) 3

2. Which tells how many in all?

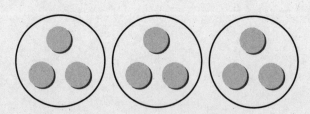

(A) 9

(B) 6

(C) 3

(D) 12

Name _____

1. Which describes the drawing shown below?

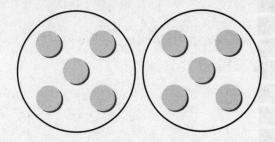

Ⓐ 2 groups of 4

Ⓑ 5 groups of 2

Ⓒ 2 groups of 3

Ⓓ 2 groups of 5

2. What equation is shown by the strip diagram?

5	5	5	5

20 pictures

Ⓐ $4 + 5 = 9$

Ⓑ $4 \times 5 = 20$

Ⓒ $20 - 5 = 15$

Ⓓ $20 + 5 = 25$

Name _____

1. What is the difference?

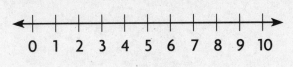

$9 - 5$

Ⓐ 4

Ⓑ 3

Ⓒ 14

Ⓓ 6

2. What is the difference?

$$\begin{array}{r} 27 \\ -\ 9 \\ \hline \end{array}$$

Ⓐ 22

Ⓑ 16

Ⓒ 36

Ⓓ 18

1. What multiplication equation does the array show?

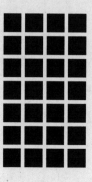

(A) 7 × 5 = 35

(B) 4 × 6 = 24

(C) 7 × 3 = 21

(D) 7 × 4 = 28

---

2. Diego has 24 stickers. He wants to put the same number of stickers on each of 6 pages in his sticker book. How many stickers will Diego put on each page?

(A) 6

(B) 3

(C) 4

(D) 8

1. Which number sentence is part of the same fact family?

$$8 + 6 = 14$$

Ⓐ $14 + 6 = 20$

Ⓑ $8 + 14 = 22$

Ⓒ $14 - 8 = 6$

Ⓓ $8 - 6 = 2$

2. What is the missing related number sentence?

$7 + 9 = 16$ $16 - 7 = 9$
$16 - 9 = 7$

Ⓐ $9 + 7 = 16$

Ⓑ $7 + 16 = 23$

Ⓒ $16 + 9 = 25$

Ⓓ $9 - 7 = 2$

1. Find the product.

$7 \times 0 = \blacksquare$

Ⓐ 8

Ⓑ 0

Ⓒ 1

Ⓓ 7

2. Find the product.

$10 \times 1 = \blacksquare$

Ⓐ 11

Ⓑ 9

Ⓒ 10

Ⓓ 100

1. Which group of numbers contains an even number?

Ⓐ 11, 27, 35

Ⓑ 49, 63, 81

Ⓒ 14, 55, 73

Ⓓ 89, 53, 97

---

2. Which group of numbers contains all odd numbers?

Ⓐ 49, 74, 96

Ⓑ 27, 55, 83

Ⓒ 16, 39, 67

Ⓓ 21, 77, 98

Name _____

1. What is the product of 2 × 8?

   (A) 16

   (B) 8

   (C) 4

   (D) 12

2. What is the missing factor?

   _____ × 6 = 12

   (A) 12

   (B) 2

   (C) 3

   (D) 9

Name _____

1. What is the product of 2 × 10?

   (A) 20

   (B) 2

   (C) 5

   (D) 10

2. What is the missing factor?

   _____ × 6 = 30

   (A) 3

   (B) 5

   (C) 9

   (D) 10

Name _____

1. What is the product of 2 × 5?

(A) 10

(B) 3

(C) 15

(D) 7

2. What is the missing factor?

_____ × 5 = 30

(A) 10

(B) 6

(C) 25

(D) 7

Name _____

1. What is the product of 3 × 10?

(A) 30

(B) 15

(C) 3

(D) 13

2. Which division equation is represented by the picture?

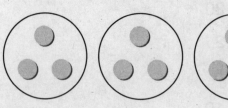

(A) 6 ÷ 2 = 3

(B) 9 − 3 = 6

(C) 9 ÷ 3 = 3

(D) 3 ÷ 3 = 1

1. Which division problem is shown on the number line?

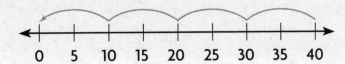

(A) 10 × 4 = 40

(B) 10 ÷ 2 = 5

(C) 30 ÷ 3 = 10

(D) 40 ÷ 10 = 4

2. Which division equation is represented by the picture?

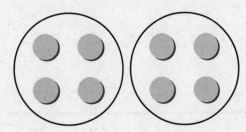

(A) 4 ÷ 2 = 2

(B) 8 ÷ 4 = 2

(C) 2 × 4 = 8

(D) 4 ÷ 4 = 1

1. Which is the unknown number?

$6 \times \blacksquare = 12$

(A) 3

(C) 2

(B) 4

(D) 6

2. Which is the product?

$6 \times 7 = \blacksquare$

(A) 42

(C) 36

(B) 13

(D) 48

1. Which is a related multiplication fact?

$14 \div 2$

(A) 2×7

(C) $7 + 7$

(B) $14 - 2$

(D) 2×6

2. Which is the product?

$7 \times 7 = \blacksquare$

(A) 35

(C) 14

(B) 49

(D) 1

Name _____

1. Which multiplication fact is shown in the array?

Ⓐ 3 × 2

Ⓑ 6 × 3

Ⓒ 3 × 5

Ⓓ 3 × 4

---

2. Which is the product?

3 × 8 = ■

Ⓐ 24

Ⓒ 36

Ⓑ 11

Ⓓ 21

Name _____

1. Which is a related multiplication fact?

9 ÷ 3

Ⓐ 3 × 3

Ⓒ 3 + 3

Ⓑ 9 − 3

Ⓓ 9 × 3

---

2. Which is the product?

9 × 4 = ■

Ⓐ 35

Ⓒ 5

Ⓑ 36

Ⓓ 13

1. Which is the unknown number?

   $4 \times \blacksquare = 12$

   Ⓐ 3

   Ⓑ 4

   Ⓒ 2

   Ⓓ 6

2. Which is the product?

   $8 \times 7 = \blacksquare$

   Ⓐ 42

   Ⓑ 13

   Ⓒ 56

   Ⓓ 48

1. What is the sum?

$$10$$
$$+\ 9$$

Ⓐ 18   Ⓒ 1

Ⓑ 19   Ⓓ 20

---

2. What is the sum?

$4 + 10 + 3$

Ⓐ 14   Ⓒ 7

Ⓑ 13   Ⓓ 17

1. What is the difference?

$$10$$
$$-\ 3$$

Ⓐ 4

Ⓑ 3

Ⓒ 7

Ⓓ 6

2. What is the difference?

$$24$$
$$-\ 10$$

Ⓐ 34

Ⓑ 4

Ⓒ 10

Ⓓ 14

1. What is the sum?

$$7 + 3$$

Ⓐ 10

Ⓑ 4

Ⓒ 11

Ⓓ 12

---

2. Which is the difference?

$$20 - 5$$

Ⓐ 25

Ⓑ 15

Ⓒ 5

Ⓓ 10

1. What is the product?

$$7 \times 6$$

Ⓐ 24

Ⓑ 42

Ⓒ 36

Ⓓ 49

2. Which has 45 as its product?

Ⓐ 4×5

Ⓑ 5×8

Ⓒ 4×9

Ⓓ 9×5

1. Three teams of 6 students play a game. How many students play the game?

   (A) 18

   (B) 12

   (C) 24

   (D) 21

2. Erica fills each plate with 5 celery sticks. There are 7 plates. How many celery sticks does Erica put on plates?

   (A) 53

   (B) 35

   (C) 42

   (D) 30

1. If this pattern continues, what is the next number?

   9, 18, 27, 36, 45, _____, …

   (A) 56

   (B) 49

   (C) 54

   (D) 48

2. Which could be the missing number in this pattern?

   7, 14, 21, 35, 42, 49, _____, 63, …

   (A) 56

   (B) 70

   (C) 65

   (D) 57

1. What is the product?

    2 × 10

  Ⓐ 12

  Ⓑ 8

  Ⓒ 20

  Ⓓ 30

2. What multiplication sentence does the array show?

  Ⓐ 2 × 4 = 8

  Ⓑ 3 × 4 = 12

  Ⓒ 2 × 3 = 6

  Ⓓ 1 × 4 = 4

1. Which figure has 4 sides and 4 vertices?

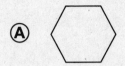

---

2. Which figure does NOT appear to have sides of equal length?

  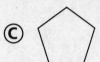

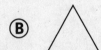 

1. Which two-dimensional figure is NOT a quadrilateral?

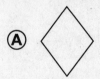

2. Which two-dimensional figure does NOT have 2 pairs of opposite sides that are parallel?

Name _____

1. Which statement best describes a trapezoid?

Ⓐ 4 right angles

Ⓑ 2 pairs of opposite sides that are parallel

Ⓒ exactly 1 pair of opposite sides that are parallel

Ⓓ 2 pairs of sides that are of equal length

---

2. Which two-dimensional shape is NOT a parallelogram?

Ⓐ square

Ⓑ rectangle

Ⓒ rhombus

Ⓓ trapezoid

Name _____

1. Which triangle appears to be the same shape as this one?

Ⓐ

Ⓑ

Ⓒ

Ⓓ

2. Which rectangle appears to be the same size as this one?

Ⓐ

Ⓑ

Ⓒ

Ⓓ

Name _____

1. Which three-dimensional shape does NOT have a curved surface?

Ⓐ

Ⓒ

Ⓑ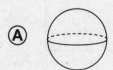

Ⓓ

---

2. Which three-dimensional shape does NOT have a flat surface?

Ⓐ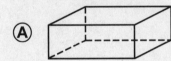

Ⓒ

Ⓑ

Ⓓ

1. It will take how many square tiles to cover this rectangle?

(A) 2   (C) 4

(B) 6   (D) 8

2. There are how many rows in this rectangle?

(A) 4   (C) 12

(B) 3   (D) 7

1. Which multiplication equation does the array represent?

(A) $4 \times 4 = 16$

(B) $5 \times 4 = 20$

(C) $5 \times 5 = 25$

(D) $4 \times 5 = 20$

2. Count to find the area of the shape. Each unit square is 1 square foot.

(A) 14 square feet   (C) 18 square feet

(B) 10 square feet   (D) 8 square feet

Name _____

1. How can you best describe the rule for the pattern below?

    3, 6, 12, 24, …

    Ⓐ Add 2.

    Ⓑ Multiply by 3.

    Ⓒ Add 3.

    Ⓓ Multiply by 2.

2. What is the next number in the pattern below?

    800, 400, 200, 100,

    Ⓐ 50

    Ⓑ 900

    Ⓒ 25

    Ⓓ 0

Name _____

1. Cassandra covered the rectangle with square tiles. How many square tiles are in the whole rectangle?

    Ⓐ 2

    Ⓑ 8

    Ⓒ 4

    Ⓓ 6

2. Which shape shows fourths?

1. What is one way you can break apart this array?

Ⓐ (3 × 2) + (3 × 1)

Ⓑ (5 × 2) + (5 × 3)

Ⓒ (3 × 2) + (3 × 3)

Ⓓ 3 × (3 + 5)

---

2. Which multiplication equation can be used to find the area of the rectangle?

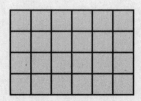

Ⓐ 4 × 6 = 24

Ⓑ 6 + 6 + 6 + 6 = 24

Ⓒ 4 × (2 + 2) = 16

Ⓓ 6 × (3 + 3) = 36

1. Find the sum.

3 + 5 + 3 + 5

Ⓐ 8

Ⓑ 16

Ⓒ 11

Ⓓ 17

2. Find the sum.

10 + 8 + 4 + 7 + 6

Ⓐ 29

Ⓑ 36

Ⓒ 35

Ⓓ 27

1. Measure to the nearest inch.

Ⓐ 4 inches

Ⓑ 5 inches

Ⓒ 3 inches

Ⓓ $3\frac{1}{2}$ inches

2. Measure to the nearest centimeter.

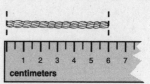

Ⓐ 4 centimeters

Ⓑ 7 centimeters

Ⓒ 6 centimeters

Ⓓ 5 centimeters

1. Four times what number equals 16?

Ⓐ 4

Ⓑ 3

Ⓒ 20

Ⓓ 12

---

2. What number plus 17 equals 26?

Ⓐ 43

Ⓑ 10

Ⓒ 8

Ⓓ 9

1. What are the missing numbers?

5, 10, ▇, 20, 25, ▇, 35

Ⓐ 11, 26   Ⓒ 15, 26

Ⓑ 15, 30   Ⓓ 40, 41

---

2. What time is shown?

Ⓐ 10:06

Ⓑ 6:42

Ⓒ 10:30

Ⓓ 6:10

---

1. Find the sum.

$$\begin{array}{r} 36 \\ + 17 \\ \hline \end{array}$$

Ⓐ 53

Ⓑ 43

Ⓒ 19

Ⓓ 63

2. Find the difference.

$$\begin{array}{r} 54 \\ - 18 \\ \hline \end{array}$$

Ⓐ 46

Ⓑ 72

Ⓒ 36

Ⓓ 26

Name _____

1. Find the elapsed time.

Start: 5:27 A.M.
End: 5:45 A.M.

Ⓐ 18 minutes

Ⓑ 72 minutes

Ⓒ 28 minutes

Ⓓ 45 minutes

2. Find the elapsed time.

Start: 10:09 P.M.
End: 10:42 P.M.

10:09

Ⓐ 51 minutes

Ⓑ 43 minutes

Ⓒ 33 minutes

Ⓓ 42 minutes

Name _____

1. Which shows how many equal parts?

Ⓐ 3

Ⓑ 8

Ⓒ 6

Ⓓ 7

2. Which shows the shaded part?

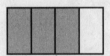

Ⓐ $\frac{3}{4}$

Ⓑ $\frac{1}{4}$

Ⓒ $\frac{1}{2}$

Ⓓ $\frac{1}{3}$

Name _____

1. Which container holds the most liquid?

Ⓐ

Ⓑ

Ⓒ

Ⓓ

2. Find the sum.

$2 + 2 + 2 + 2$

Ⓐ 4

Ⓑ 2

Ⓒ 8

Ⓓ 6

Name _____

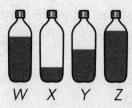

W X Y Z

1. Which bottle of water has the least amount of water?

Ⓐ Bottle *X*

Ⓑ Bottle *Z*

Ⓒ Bottle *W*

Ⓓ Bottle *Y*

2. Which bottle of water has the most amount of water?

Ⓐ Bottle *X*

Ⓑ Bottle *Z*

Ⓒ Bottle *W*

Ⓓ Bottle *Y*

1. Which would weigh the most?

Ⓐ

Ⓑ

Ⓒ

Ⓓ

2. Find the sum.

16 + 16 + 16

Ⓐ 32

Ⓑ 318

Ⓒ 48

Ⓓ 46

1. Which two balances show that the objects have the same mass?

A

B

C

D

Ⓐ A and C

Ⓑ B and C

Ⓒ C and D

Ⓓ B and D

2. Which would weigh the least?

Ⓐ lion

Ⓑ stapler

Ⓒ paper clip

Ⓓ bowling ball

1. What number do the tally marks show?

Ⓐ 5

Ⓑ 8

Ⓒ 3

Ⓓ 7

2. What is the difference?

$$\begin{array}{r} 19 \\ -\ 7 \\ \hline \end{array}$$

Ⓐ 13

Ⓑ 2

Ⓒ 12

Ⓓ 26

Use the Favorite Season table.

1. How many students chose summer?

Ⓐ 10

Ⓑ 3

Ⓒ 7

Ⓓ 8

Favorite Season	
Season	**Tally**
Spring	卌 IIII
Summer	卌 III
Fall	IIII
Winter	卌 II

2. Which season got the most votes?

Ⓐ Spring

Ⓑ Summer

Ⓒ Fall

Ⓓ Winter

Name _____

1. What is the sum?

$$15 + 12 + 5$$

Ⓐ 27

Ⓑ 20

Ⓒ 17

Ⓓ 32

2. What is the difference?

$$40 - 12$$

Ⓐ 52

Ⓑ 26

Ⓒ 28

Ⓓ 38

✂ -

Name _____

Use the Number of Books Students Read table.

1. How many books did students read in November?

Ⓐ 10

Ⓑ 8

Ⓒ 5

Ⓓ 7

Number of Books Students Read	
Month	**Tally**
September	JHT II
October	JHT JHT II
November	JHT III
December	JHT

2. How many more books did the students read in October than November?

Ⓐ 2

Ⓒ 4

Ⓑ 5

Ⓓ 8

1. Which number names point *A* on the number line?

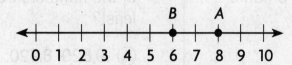

Ⓐ 7

Ⓑ 9

Ⓒ 8

Ⓓ 6

Jeremy took a survey of his classmates to find out their favorite farm animal. The results are shown in the table at the right.

Favorite Farm Animal	
Animal	**Tally**
chicken	IIII
cow	IIII III
goat	IIII I
horse	IIII IIII II

2. Which farm animal did the most students choose?

Ⓐ chicken

Ⓑ cow

Ⓒ goat

Ⓓ horse

1. Lionel earns $12 an hour. How much does he earn for 5 hours of work?

   (A) $84

   (B) $17

   (C) $60

   (D) $72

2. Which shows the correct order of the numbers from greatest to least?

   (A) 9,820; 8,920; 9,920; 920

   (B) 9,920; 9,820; 8,920; 920

   (C) 8,920; 9,920; 9,820; 920

   (D) 920; 8,920; 9,820; 9,920

1. Which is 2,378 rounded to the nearest hundred?

   (A) 2,300

   (B) 2,400

   (C) 2,380

   (D) 2,000

2. Which shows the numbers in order from least to greatest?

   (A) 85,723; 85,332; 8,573; 8,000

   (B) 85,723; 8,573; 85,332; 8,000

   (C) 8,573; 8,000; 85,332; 85,723

   (D) 8,000; 8,573; 85,332; 85,723

1. Marco saves $6 a week. How much money does he save in 11 weeks?

   Ⓐ $99

   Ⓑ $60

   Ⓒ $66

   Ⓓ $121

2. If Madison wants to save $72 in 6 weeks, how much should she save each week?

   Ⓐ $8

   Ⓑ $10

   Ⓒ $9

   Ⓓ $12

1. At the office supply store, Jocelyn buys a binder, which costs $4, and 3 pens, each of which costs $3. How much does Jocelyn spend?

   Ⓐ $9

   Ⓑ $7

   Ⓒ $5

   Ⓓ $13

2. Sean printed 40 flyers to distribute at his lacrosse game. He kept 4 flyers and gave an equal number to 4 players to pass out. How many flyers did each player pass out?

   Ⓐ 10

   Ⓑ 36

   Ⓒ 9

   Ⓓ 8

1. What is the sum?

20 + 20

Ⓐ 50

Ⓑ 400

Ⓒ 40

Ⓓ 30

2. Which is the next number in the pattern shown below?

5, 10, 15, 20, 25, ___

Ⓐ 30   Ⓒ 50

Ⓑ 26   Ⓓ 35

1. Which is the answer to 150 + 20 − 50?

Ⓐ 170   Ⓒ 220

Ⓑ 120   Ⓓ 100

2. Which is the product of 16 × 5?

Ⓐ 530   Ⓒ 80

Ⓑ 50   Ⓓ 30

Write the correct answer.

1. What is another way to write
   20 + 6?

   _____

Use the numbers in the box for 2–3.

1,075	950	876

2. Which number is greater than
   1,000?

   _____

3. Which number is less than 900?

   _____

4. What number names the point on
   the number line?

   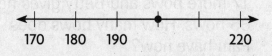

   _____

Use the numbers in the box for 5–6.

759	1,043	1,069

5. Which number makes the
   comparison true?

   1,183 > 986 > ▓

   _____

6. Which could be the unknown
   number?

   784 < 1,052 < ▓

   _____

7. Carmen has 3 pizzas that are the
   same size. She cuts the cheese
   pizza into 6 equal slices, the
   mushroom pizza into 4 equal
   slices, and the sausage pizza into
   12 equal slices. Which pizza has
   the largest slices?

   _____

GO ON ➡

8. What is a name for the equal parts in the shape?

_____

11. Which shape shows thirds?

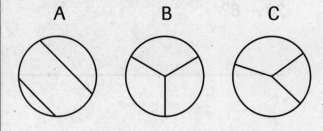

A   B   C

_____

9. Bristol has 2 loaves of bread that are the same size. She cuts each loaf into four equal pieces and uses 6 pieces.

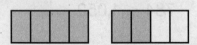

How much bread did Bristol use?

_____
_____

12. Jess saw 7 deer in the morning. In the afternoon, Jess saw double that number. How many deer did Jess see in the afternoon?

_____

13. What tens fact can you use to find 15 − 7?

_____

10. What number goes in the box?

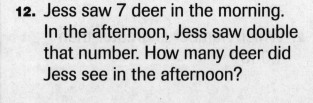

$$26 \rightarrow 20 + 6$$
$$\underline{+\ 38} \rightarrow \underline{30 + 8}$$
$$50 + 14 = \blacksquare$$

_____

14. Pam has 44 bows. She makes 17 more bows and Betty gives her 35 bows. How many bows does Pam have now?

_____

GO ON ➡

15. On Saturday, Kevin slept 9 hours. There are 24 hours in a day. How many hours was Kevin awake on Saturday?

_____

16. Mr. Brown has a box of 75 markers. He gives 16 markers to his students. How many markers does Mr. Brown have now?

_____

17. There are 46 students on a playground. Of these, 28 are girls and the rest are boys. What number sentence can you use to find how many of the students are boys?

_____

18. There are 245 hardcover books and 550 paperback books in a bookstore. More paperback books are delivered to the store. Now there are 995 books. How many books are delivered to the store?

_____

19. There are 216 people at a dog show. Then 472 more people come. What number sentence can you use to find the number of people at the dog show now?

_____

20. There are 322 fans at the soccer field on Wednesday and 228 fans on Thursday. What number sentence can you use to find the number of fans at the soccer field on both days?

_____

21. Amy buys a bag of popcorn with these coins. How much does the bag of popcorn cost if she does not receive any change?

_____

GO ON

22. Isabel has these coins. What is the total value of the coins?

_____

23. Gary has 8 plates. He puts 3 waffles on each plate. How many waffles are on the plates?

_____

24. There are 14 balloons. Each child gets 2 balloons. How many children are there?

_____

25. There are an even number of kittens and an odd number of puppies in a pet store. Write the number of kittens and the number of puppies that might be at the pet store.

_____

26. There are 350 rubber bands in a bag. There are 100 fewer rubber bands in Mr. Stuart's desk. How many rubber bands are in Mr. Stuart's desk?

_____

Write a number sentence with a ▆ **for the missing number for 27–28. Then solve.**

27. Katy drew 25 hearts on a notebook. Rita drew some hearts too. They drew 39 hearts altogether. How many hearts did Rita draw?

_____

28. Mr. Troy's students made 43 pictures in class. Some of the pictures were on the wall and 24 were in folders. How many pictures were on the wall?

_____

GO ON

29. How many vertices does this shape have?

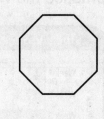

_____

30. A box has 6 faces, 12 edges, and 8 vertices. What could be the shape of the box?

_____

31. How many of these shapes have exactly 6 vertices?

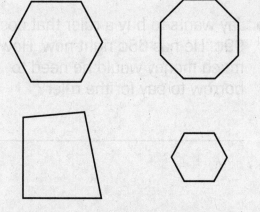

_____

32. Use an inch ruler. What is the length of the eraser to the nearest inch?

_____

33. Emily uses color tiles to make a rectangle. She uses 6 rows of tiles and 5 columns of tiles. How many tiles does Emily use?

_____

34. Tamara has two colors of string. If the black string is 4 inches long, about how long is the gray string?

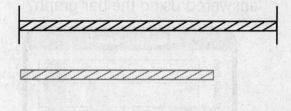

_____

GO ON

35. Jan gets to school at the time shown on the clock. What time does Jan get to school?

_____

36. What is a question that can be answered using the pictograph?

Pets We Have	
Cat	☺ ☺ ☺ ☺
Fish	☺ ☺
Gerbil	☺
Dog	☺ ☺ ☺ ☺ ☺

_____

37. What is a question that can be answered using the bar graph?

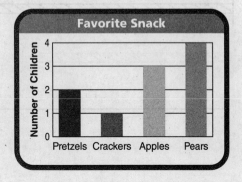

_____

38. Use the bar graph. What is a good prediction for how many days Joe might practice the viola in week 5?

_____

39. Jim has $19 in the bank. Then he withdraws $6. How much money does Jim have in the bank now?

_____

40. Jay wants to buy a ruler that costs 99¢. He has 65¢ right now. How much money would he need to borrow to pay for the ruler?

_____

Fill in the bubble for the correct answer.

1. Evan has 54 pencils. He places the same number of pencils in each of 6 pencil cases. Which related fact shows the number of pencils in each pencil case?

   Ⓐ 3 × 18 = 54

   Ⓑ 50 ÷ 5 = 10

   Ⓒ 54 ÷ 18 = 3

   Ⓓ 9 × 6 = 54

2. Mari is drawing a sketch for a flower garden. Each unit square is 1 square foot.

   Which multiplication equation can be used to find the area of the flower garden?

   Ⓐ 4 + 5 = 9

   Ⓑ 4 × 5 = 20

   Ⓒ 4 × 4 = 16

   Ⓓ 4 × 6 = 24

3. Carmen is putting tape around the edge of a poster. The poster has side lengths of 3 feet and 4 feet. How many feet of tape will Carmen need?

   Ⓐ 14 feet

   Ⓑ 7 feet

   Ⓒ 6 feet

   Ⓓ 12 feet

4. Mr. Bonta ate the part of a pie that is shaded. What fraction of the pie did he eat?

   Ⓐ $\frac{1}{6}$ Ⓒ $\frac{3}{6}$

   Ⓑ $\frac{5}{6}$ Ⓓ $\frac{4}{6}$

5. Devin earns $8 per hour at a bakery. How much does he earn in 9 hours?

   Ⓐ $64   Ⓒ $81

   Ⓑ $17   Ⓓ $72

GO ON

6. The number of people attending a baseball game is 1,402. Which model shows the number 1,402?

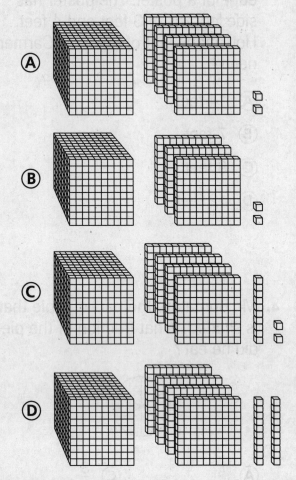

Ⓐ

Ⓑ

Ⓒ

Ⓓ

7. Which set of numbers contains all odd numbers?

Ⓐ 211, 469, 788

Ⓑ 331, 977, 456

Ⓒ 323, 542, 901

Ⓓ 503, 217, 851

8. Which fraction names the point closest to 0 on the number line?

```
<---|---|---|---|--->
    0           1
```

Ⓐ $\frac{2}{4}$

Ⓑ $\frac{4}{4}$

Ⓒ $\frac{1}{4}$

Ⓓ $\frac{3}{4}$

9. There are 2 barns on a horse ranch. Each barn has 4 rows of horse stalls. There are 20 stalls in each row. The Commutative Property can help you multiply. Which shows the Commutative Property?

Ⓐ $2 \times 4 \times 20 = (2 \times 4) \times 20$

Ⓑ $2 \times 4 \times 20 = 2 \times 4 \times 20$

Ⓒ $2 \times 4 \times 20 = 2 \times 20 \times 4$

Ⓓ $2 \times 4 \times 20 = (2 \times 4 \times 20)$

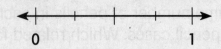

GO ON

10. Carter starts practicing piano at 3:45 P.M. He finishes 30 minutes later. At what time does he finish?

(A) 4:15 P.M. (C) 3:10 P.M.

(B) 3:15 P.M. (D) 4:45 P.M.

11. Jack finished $\frac{3}{8}$ of his math problems. Which shows $\frac{3}{8}$ written as a sum of unit fractions?

(A) $\frac{1}{8} + \frac{2}{8}$

(B) $\frac{1}{8} + \frac{1}{8} + \frac{1}{8}$

(C) $\frac{3}{8} + \frac{3}{8} + \frac{3}{8}$

(D) $\frac{1}{4} + \frac{1}{8}$

12. Deena gets a $20 allowance every month. She has a savings plan in which she saves $7 of her allowance each month. How much will she save in 5 months?

(A) $27 (C) $35

(B) $65 (D) $100

13. Katherine wants to buy 2 books. Each book costs $14. She has $20 saved and will borrow the rest of the money from her sister. Katherine will pay her sister back $4 each week. How many weeks will it take to pay back her sister?

Record your answer and fill in the bubbles on the grid. Be sure to use the correct place value.

⓪	⓪	⓪	.
①	①	①	
②	②	②	
③	③	③	
④	④	④	
⑤	⑤	⑤	
⑥	⑥	⑥	
⑦	⑦	⑦	
⑧	⑧	⑧	
⑨	⑨	⑨	

14. Drew has 53 trading cards. He gives 18 to his brother. How many trading cards does he have left?

18	

53

(A) 35

(B) 71

(C) 37

(D) 33

GO ON

15. Brett stacked 15 boxes of markers. He places his stacks in 3 rows. If each row has the same number of boxes, how many boxes are in each row?

(A) 4   (B) 3   (C) 5   (D) 6

16. Brooke folds her socks in sets of 2. She folds 18 socks. How many sets of socks does she fold?

(A) 10   (B) 8   (C) 6   (D) 9

17. Ricardo has the money shown.

How much money does Ricardo have?

(A) $20.40   (C) $24.60

(B) $24.40   (D) $24.55

18. Which measurement unit should be used for the volume of the container?

(A) pounds   (C) inches

(B) liters   (D) grams

19. The diagram shows the outline of a vegetable garden. Each unit square is 1 square foot.

What is the area of the vegetable garden in square feet?

Record your answer and fill in the bubbles on the grid. Be sure to use the correct place value.

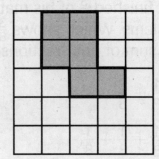

GO ON

20. Adam has 3 packages to mail. Their weights are 21 pounds, 24 pounds, and 12 pounds. What is the total weight of the packages?

Ⓐ 43 pounds Ⓒ 57 pounds

Ⓑ 59 pounds Ⓓ 36 pounds

21. Jasmine has 8 orchid plants. Each plant has 3 flowers on it.

0 3 6 9 12 15 18 21 24 27 30

How many orchids does Jasmine have in all?

Ⓐ 24 Ⓑ 16 Ⓒ 21 Ⓓ 11

22. Justin puts 5 red blocks, 5 green blocks, and 5 blue blocks in a bag. Which multiplication sentence shows how many blocks he puts in the bag in all?

Ⓐ 3 × 3 = 9

Ⓑ 5 × 4 = 20

Ⓒ 3 × 4 = 12

Ⓓ 3 × 5 = 15

23. Alana buys 8 oranges. Each orange weighs 8 ounces. How many pounds do the oranges weigh in all?

Ⓐ 64 Ⓑ 4 Ⓒ 16 Ⓓ 5

24. Deondra divided this rectangle into 4 parts with equal area. What is the area of each part?

Ⓐ 14 square units

Ⓑ 15 square units

Ⓒ 12 square units

Ⓓ 16 square units

25. A toy bear has 4 buttons. How many buttons do 8 bears have?

Record your answer and fill in the bubbles on the grid. Be sure to use the correct place value.

⓪	⓪	⓪	.
①	①	①	
②	②	②	
③	③	③	
④	④	④	
⑤	⑤	⑤	
⑥	⑥	⑥	
⑦	⑦	⑦	
⑧	⑧	⑧	
⑨	⑨	⑨	

GO ON

26. William divides a flower box into 8 equal sections. What fraction names one section of the flower box?

(A) $\frac{2}{8}$

(C) $\frac{1}{8}$

(B) $\frac{4}{8}$

(D) $\frac{8}{1}$

27. Landon has 24 slices of pumpkin bread. He saves 6 slices for his family. Then he gives 2 slices of the remaining bread to each person at a picnic until all the slices are gone. To how many people does Landon give pumpkin bread?

(A) 16

(B) 8

(C) 10

(D) 9

28. The state of Texas is 696,241 square kilometers. Which digit in 696,241 is in the thousands place?

(A) 2

(B) 6

(C) 4

(D) 9

29. Diego needs 4 nails for each picture frame. How many nails does he need for 5 picture frames?

Picture Frames	1	2	3	4	5
Nails	4	8	12	16	

(A) 20

(B) 19

(C) 16

(D) 18

30. James and Steffi each have graham crackers divided into fourths. James eats $\frac{3}{4}$ of his and Steffi eats $\frac{2}{4}$ of hers. Which statement is true?

James   Steffi

(A) $\frac{2}{4} > \frac{3}{4}$

(B) $\frac{2}{4} = \frac{3}{4}$

(C) $\frac{3}{4} < \frac{2}{4}$

(D) $\frac{3}{4} > \frac{2}{4}$

GO ON

31. Valeria colored $\frac{4}{6}$ of a rectangle.

How many thirds of the rectangle did she color?

Ⓐ $\frac{1}{3}$ Ⓒ $\frac{3}{1}$

Ⓑ $\frac{2}{3}$ Ⓓ $\frac{3}{3}$

32. A class of 36 students is divided into 6 teams, with the same number of students on each team. How many students are on each team?

Ⓐ 7   Ⓒ 8

Ⓑ 5   Ⓓ 6

33. A rock collector has 1,357 agates, 1,347 crystals, 1,308 sandstone rocks, and 1,341 limestone rocks in his collection. Of which kind of rock does he have the greatest number?

Ⓐ agates   Ⓒ sandstone

Ⓑ crystals   Ⓓ limestone

34. Brandon hiked $\frac{3}{4}$ of a mile.

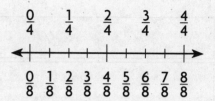

Which fraction is equivalent to $\frac{3}{4}$?

Ⓐ $\frac{3}{8}$

Ⓑ $\frac{6}{8}$

Ⓒ $\frac{4}{8}$

Ⓓ $\frac{5}{8}$

35. Melanie has 222 red marbles and 118 green marbles. About how many more red marbles does she have than green marbles?

Ⓐ 100

Ⓑ 300

Ⓒ 200

Ⓓ 400

GO ON

36. Four friends share 2 granola bars equally.

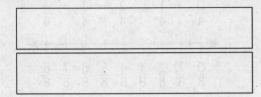

How much of a granola bar does each friend get?

(A) $\frac{1}{9}$

(B) $\frac{1}{3}$

(C) $\frac{1}{2}$

(D) $\frac{1}{6}$

37. Addison biked for 52 minutes on Saturday. This was 18 more minutes than she biked on Friday. How many minutes did she bike on Friday?

Record your answer and fill in the bubbles on the grid. Be sure to use the correct place value.

.			.
⓪	⓪	⓪	
①	①	①	
②	②	②	
③	③	③	
④	④	④	
⑤	⑤	⑤	
⑥	⑥	⑥	
⑦	⑦	⑦	
⑧	⑧	⑧	
⑨	⑨	⑨	

38. Ellie swims 8 laps. Camila swims 4 times as many laps as Ellie. Which expression represents the number of laps Camila swims?

(A) $4 + 8$ (C) $8 + 8 + 8$

(B) 4×8 (D) 4×2

39. A dolphin has 4 fins. How many fins do 8 dolphins have?

(A) 12   (C) 24

(B) 16   (D) 32

40. Which three-dimensional solid has 5 faces?

(A)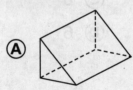

(B)

(C)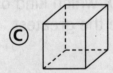

(D)

GO ON

41. Between which two thousands is 6,889 on the number line?

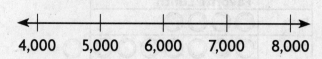

- Ⓐ 7,000 and 8,000
- Ⓑ 4,000 and 5,000
- Ⓒ 6,000 and 7,000
- Ⓓ 5,000 and 6,000

42. Sofia's family drives 248 miles Tuesday and 264 miles Wednesday. Which correctly compares the two numbers?

248 ⬤ 264

- Ⓐ >
- Ⓒ =
- Ⓑ <
- Ⓓ −

43. Calvin buys a book. Which word describes his decision?

- Ⓐ saving
- Ⓑ spending
- Ⓒ credit
- Ⓓ giving

44. David drew these quadrilaterals.

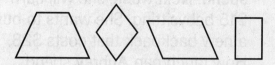

How many parallelograms did he draw?

- Ⓐ 4
- Ⓒ 2
- Ⓑ 1
- Ⓓ 3

45. Logan has 5 bags of shells. Each bag has 5 large shells and 2 small shells. How many shells does Logan have in all?

- Ⓐ 25
- Ⓒ 35
- Ⓑ 50
- Ⓓ 27

46. Xavier drew a number line.

Which fraction names point *G*?

- Ⓐ $\frac{3}{8}$
- Ⓒ $\frac{1}{8}$
- Ⓑ $\frac{2}{8}$
- Ⓓ $\frac{5}{8}$

GO ON

47. Aubrey's older sister has $15 to spend. Next week, she will earn $15 babysitting. She wants to buy a new backpack that costs $28. How much can Aubrey spend today if she plans to buy the backpack after babysitting next week?

(A) $5   (C) $15

(B) $2   (D) $30

48. Toy figures of arctic animals are for sale in a store. The animals that the store has fewer of have a higher price. The table shows the price for each toy.

Arctic Animal Figures	
Type of Animal	**Price**
Polar bear	$5
Arctic fox	$2
Seal	$3
Whale	$9

Of which of the toys does the store have the fewest?

(A) Polar bear

(B) Arctic fox

(C) Seal

(D) Whale

Use the pictograph for 49–50.

Favorite Lunch	
Pasta	○○○○
Pizza	○○○○○○○
Sandwich	○○○
Taco	

○ = 2 votes.

49. How many more students chose pizza than sandwich?

(A) 4

(B) 3

(C) 8

(D) 6

50. How many students chose pasta?

(A) 8

(B) 4

(C) 3

(D) 6

STOP

Fill in the bubble for the correct answer.

1. Isabella has 40 paper clips. She places the same number of paper clips in each of 8 envelopes. Which related fact shows the number of paper clips in each envelope?

   Ⓐ 8 × 5 = 40

   Ⓑ 40 ÷ 4 = 10

   Ⓒ 40 ÷ 10 = 4

   Ⓓ 4 × 10 = 40

2. Angel is drawing a sketch for a painting. Each unit square is 1 square inch.

   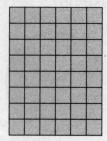

   Which equation can be used to find the area of the painting?

   Ⓐ 8 + 6 = 14

   Ⓑ 8 × 5 = 40

   Ⓒ 8 × 6 = 48

   Ⓓ 7 × 6 = 42

3. Ava is gluing a ribbon around a picture frame. The frame has side lengths of 5 inches and 8 inches. How many inches of ribbon will Ava use?

   Ⓐ 12 inches

   Ⓑ 40 inches

   Ⓒ 13 inches

   Ⓓ 26 inches

4. Joseph colored part of a circle.

   What fraction of the circle did he color?

   Ⓐ $\frac{1}{4}$ Ⓑ $\frac{3}{4}$ Ⓒ $\frac{4}{4}$ Ⓓ $\frac{2}{4}$

5. Mr. Ortiz earns $9 per hour working at a restaurant. How much does he earn in 5 hours?

   Ⓐ $14   Ⓒ $45

   Ⓑ $40   Ⓓ $4

GO ON

6. The number of students in Kimberly's school is 1,154. Which shows another way to write the number 1,154?

Ⓐ 1,000 + 100 + 50 + 40

Ⓑ 1,000 + 100 + 50 + 4

Ⓒ 1,000 + 15 + 4

Ⓓ 1,000 + 50 + 4

7. Which set of numbers contains all even numbers?

Ⓐ 336, 484, 952

Ⓑ 347, 188, 246

Ⓒ 178, 218, 345

Ⓓ 908, 955, 942

8. Which fraction names the point closest to 0 on the number line?

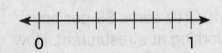

Ⓐ $\frac{6}{8}$ Ⓒ $\frac{5}{8}$

Ⓑ $\frac{7}{8}$ Ⓓ $\frac{4}{8}$

9. There are 5 stands at a farmer's market. Each stand has 30 baskets of vegetables. How many baskets of vegetables are at the farmer's market?

Ⓐ 200

Ⓑ 150

Ⓒ 160

Ⓓ 80

10. Emma leaves for school at 7:50 A.M. She eats breakfast 30 minutes before she leaves and wakes up 15 minutes before she eats breakfast. What time does Emma wake up?

Ⓐ 7:15 A.M.

Ⓑ 7:35 A.M.

Ⓒ 7:05 A.M.

Ⓓ 8:05 A.M.

GO ON ➡

11. Which fraction is represented by the sum of these unit fractions?

$$\frac{1}{4} + \frac{1}{4} + \frac{1}{4}$$

(A) $\frac{3}{4}$ (B) $\frac{2}{4}$ (C) $\frac{1}{4}$ (D) $\frac{4}{1}$

12. Brianna earns $20 babysitting every week. She has a savings plan in which she saves $5 each week. How much will she save in 6 weeks?

(A) $100   (C) $25

(B) $15   (D) $30

13. Davis wants to buy 8 songs online. Each song costs $2. He has $10 saved and will borrow the rest of the money from his mother. Davis will pay his mother back $2 each week. How many weeks will it take to pay back his mother?

Record your answer and fill in the bubbles on the grid. Be sure to use the correct place value.

⊙	⊙	⊙	.
⓪	⓪	⓪	
①	①	①	
②	②	②	
③	③	③	
④	④	④	
⑤	⑤	⑤	
⑥	⑥	⑥	
⑦	⑦	⑦	
⑧	⑧	⑧	
⑨	⑨	⑨	

14. Alex has 48 photos of a trip in one album and 36 photos of the same trip in another album.

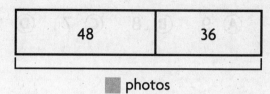

☐ photos

How many photos of his trip does he have in the two albums?

(A) 74

(B) 84

(C) 82

(D) 12

15. Caleb has 35 stamps. He places 5 stamps on each page of a book. How many pages does he use?

(A) 7

(B) 30

(C) 8

(D) 6

GO ON

16. Ian has 1 basket. There are 8 apples in the basket. How many apples does Ian have?

(A) 9   (B) 8   (C) 7   (D) 10

17. Trinity has this money in her pocket.

How much money does Trinity have?

(A) $5   (C) $13

(B) $25   (D) $7

18. Which measurement unit should be used for the weight of the golf ball?

(A) pounds

(B) liters

(C) inches

(D) ounces

19. The diagram shows the outline of a backyard pond. Each unit square is 1 square foot.

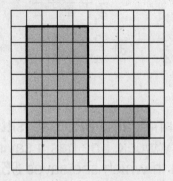

What is the area of the backyard pond?

Record your answer and fill in the bubbles on the grid. Be sure to use the correct place value.

(0)	(0)	(0)	.
(1)	(1)	(1)	
(2)	(2)	(2)	
(3)	(3)	(3)	
(4)	(4)	(4)	
(5)	(5)	(5)	
(6)	(6)	(6)	
(7)	(7)	(7)	
(8)	(8)	(8)	
(9)	(9)	(9)	

20. Taya runs a 200-meter race. Len runs a 400-meter race. Sam runs 500 fewer meters than Taya and Len together. How many meters does Sam run?

(A) 100   (C) 200

(B) 400   (D) 600

GO ON →

21. Francisco has 3 puppies. The puppies each have 3 tags on their collars. Which shows how many tags the puppies have altogether?

Ⓐ 3 + 3

Ⓑ 2 + 3

Ⓒ 3 + 3 + 3

Ⓓ 3 + 1

22. Christina has 12 pictures. Which describes one array Christina could make using all of her pictures?

Ⓐ 3 rows of 4

Ⓑ 4 rows of 2

Ⓒ 6 rows of 6

Ⓓ 4 rows of 8

23. Which tool would you use to measure the mass of a pineapple?

Ⓐ measuring cup

Ⓑ ruler

Ⓒ balance

Ⓓ thermometer

24. Damian is painting his room. He divides one wall into 6 equal sections. If he paints one section, what fraction of the wall does he paint?

Ⓐ $\frac{1}{6}$

Ⓑ $\frac{6}{1}$

Ⓒ $\frac{1}{12}$

Ⓓ $\frac{1}{4}$

25. Molly has 36 stickers. She puts 9 stickers on each page in a sticker book. How many pages does she use?

Record your answer and fill in the bubbles on the grid. Be sure to use the correct place value.

⓪	⓪	⓪	.
①	①	①	
②	②	②	
③	③	③	
④	④	④	
⑤	⑤	⑤	
⑥	⑥	⑥	
⑦	⑦	⑦	
⑧	⑧	⑧	
⑨	⑨	⑨	

GO ON

26. Jesse divides a game board into 4 equal sections for the game he is making. What fraction names one section of the game board?

Ⓐ $\frac{1}{4}$

Ⓑ $\frac{3}{4}$

Ⓒ $\frac{2}{4}$

Ⓓ $\frac{4}{4}$

27. Elijah has 40 pieces of paper. He takes 4 pieces. Then he hands 4 pieces to each of his classmates until they are gone. To how many classmates does Elijah give pieces of paper?

Ⓐ 8

Ⓑ 4

Ⓒ 9

Ⓓ 10

28. The population of Mission, Texas, in 2011 was 79,368. Which digit in 79,368 is in the hundreds place?

Ⓐ 7

Ⓑ 9

Ⓒ 6

Ⓓ 3

29. It costs $8 to rent a bicycle for one hour. How much will it cost for Josie and her 4 friends to rent bicycles for one hour?

Ⓐ $32

Ⓑ $40

Ⓒ $13

Ⓓ $12

30. Sadie and Ruby had equal-size pears. Sadie ate $\frac{3}{4}$ of her pear. Ruby ate $\frac{3}{6}$ of her pear. Which statement about their pears is true?

Ⓐ Sadie ate more than Ruby.

Ⓑ Sadie and Ruby ate the same amount.

Ⓒ Ruby ate more than Sadie.

Ⓓ There is no way to determine who ate more of her pear.

GO ON

31. Estella read for $\frac{1}{2}$ hour.

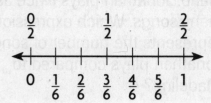

Which fraction is equivalent to $\frac{1}{2}$?

Ⓐ $\frac{3}{6}$

Ⓑ $\frac{2}{6}$

Ⓒ $\frac{1}{6}$

Ⓓ $\frac{5}{6}$

32. Mariana has 3 bowls. Each bowl has 9 grapes. How many grapes does she have in all?

Ⓐ 12

Ⓑ 27

Ⓒ 24

Ⓓ 30

33. The populations of three cities are 12,578, 12,534, and 12,509. Which shows these numbers in order from greatest to least?

Ⓐ 12,534; 12,578; 12,509

Ⓑ 12,509; 12,534; 12,578

Ⓒ 12,534; 12,509; 12,578

Ⓓ 12,578; 12,534; 12,509

34. Brandon hiked $\frac{1}{3}$ of a mile.

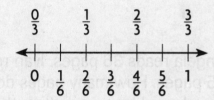

Which fraction is equivalent to $\frac{1}{3}$?

Ⓐ $\frac{3}{6}$ Ⓒ $\frac{2}{6}$

Ⓑ $\frac{5}{6}$ Ⓓ $\frac{1}{6}$

35. Edith has 87 animal stickers and 32 sports stickers. About how many stickers does she have in all?

Ⓐ 50   Ⓒ 130

Ⓑ 150   Ⓓ 120

GO ON

36. Six friends share 2 oranges equally.

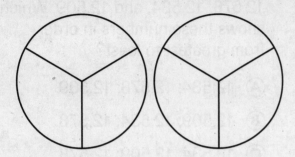

What fraction of an orange does each friend get?

(A) $\frac{1}{3}$　　　(C) $\frac{1}{2}$

(B) $\frac{1}{4}$　　　(D) $\frac{1}{6}$

37. Angela reads 36 pages. Ivan reads 45 pages. How many pages do Angela and Ivan read altogether?

Record your answer and fill in the bubbles on the grid. Be sure to use the correct place value.

⓪ ⓪ ⓪ .
① ① ①
② ② ②
③ ③ ③
④ ④ ④
⑤ ⑤ ⑤
⑥ ⑥ ⑥
⑦ ⑦ ⑦
⑧ ⑧ ⑧
⑨ ⑨ ⑨

38. Madeline plays 4 songs on the piano. Jonathan plays twice as many songs. Which expression represents the number of songs Jonathan plays compared to Madeline?

(A) $4 + 2$　　　(C) $4 + 4 + 4$

(B) 3×4　　　(D) 4×2

39. Marty has 3 cups that each have 6 marbles. Which division fact helps you to know how many marbles Marty has in all?

(A) $18 \div 6$　　　(C) $24 \div 3$

(B) $18 \div 9$　　　(D) $24 \div 8$

40. Which three-dimensional solid has 1 vertex?

(A) 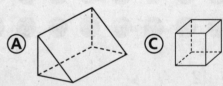　　　(C)

(B) 　　　(D)

GO ON

41. Mabel's mom biked 4,187 miles in one year. What is this number rounded to the nearest thousand?

(A) 5,000   (C) 3,000

(B) 4,000   (D) 2,000

42. Mr. Carson has 158 pieces of red paper, 241 pieces of green paper, 197 pieces of yellow paper, and 207 pieces of orange paper in his art center. Of which color does he have the most pieces of paper?

(A) orange

(B) red

(C) green

(D) yellow

43. Miranda gives money to a food bank. Which word describes her decision?

(A) saving

(B) spending

(C) credit

(D) giving

44. Aaliya drew these quadrilaterals.

How many trapezoids did she draw?

(A) 3   (C) 2

(B) 1   (D) 4

45. Keesha has 32 foam balls. She takes 4 balls to play a game. She places the rest in bags that each hold 4 balls. How many bags does she use?

(A) 7   (C) 4

(B) 8   (D) 16

46. Helena drew a number line.

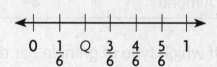

Which fraction names point Q?

(A) $\frac{3}{6}$ (C) $\frac{1}{6}$

(B) $\frac{2}{6}$ (D) $\frac{4}{6}$

GO ON

47. Kylie has $12. She wants to save $18 to buy an art set. She spends $5 on a book. How much money does she need to save to buy the art set?

Ⓐ $13   Ⓒ $7

Ⓑ $30   Ⓓ $11

48. A store sells different flavors of granola bars. The store has fewer of some granola bars and charges more for them. The table shows the price for each flavor of granola bar.

Granola Bars	
Flavor	Price per box
Chocolate	$3
Peanut butter	$4
Coconut	$6
Almond	$4

Of which type of granola bar does the store have the most?

Ⓐ Chocolate

Ⓑ Peanut butter

Ⓒ Coconut

Ⓓ Almond

Use the dot plot for 49–50.

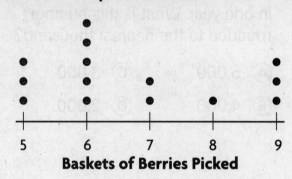

Baskets of Berries Picked

49. How many more people picked 6 baskets of berries than 7 or 8 baskets combined?

Ⓐ 3

Ⓑ 2

Ⓒ 4

Ⓓ 5

50. What is the number of baskets picked by the least number of people?

Ⓐ 7

Ⓑ 4

Ⓒ 5

Ⓓ 8

STOP

Fill in the bubble for the correct answer.

1. Robert has 18 board games. He puts the same number of board games in each of 3 drawers. Which related fact shows the number of board games in each drawer?

   (A) $8 \times 3 = 24$

   (B) $18 \div 9 = 2$

   (C) $18 \div 3 = 6$

   (D) $2 \times 9 = 18$

3. Ryan is building a wood fence around a garden. The garden has side lengths of 9 feet and 7 feet. How many feet of fence will Ryan use?

   (A) 14 feet

   (B) 32 feet

   (C) 18 feet

   (D) 63 feet

2. Zach draws a sketch of a hamster playhouse. Each unit square is 1 square inch.

   Which multiplication equation can be used to find the area of the playhouse?

   (A) $4 \times 7 = 28$

   (B) $8 \times 4 = 32$

   (C) $3 \times 7 = 21$

   (D) $4 \times 6 = 24$

4. What fraction of the flowers are shaded?

   (A) $\dfrac{3}{3}$ (C) $\dfrac{3}{1}$

   (B) $\dfrac{2}{3}$ (D) $\dfrac{1}{3}$

5. Adrian earns $7 per hour helping at a ranch. How much does he earn in 6 hours?

   (A) $13   (C) $45

   (B) $42   (D) $48

GO ON

6. Danielle drew this quick picture to show the number of bean plants in a field.

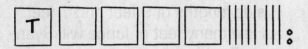

How many bean plants are in the field?

Ⓐ 1,248   Ⓒ 1,428

Ⓑ 1,842   Ⓓ 1,482

7. Which set of numbers contains all odd numbers?

Ⓐ 148, 309, 417

Ⓑ 948, 564, 306

Ⓒ 201, 143, 157

Ⓓ 465, 233, 688

8. Which fraction names the point farthest from 0 on the number line?

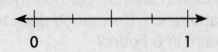

Ⓐ $\frac{3}{4}$ Ⓑ $\frac{4}{4}$ Ⓒ $\frac{1}{4}$ Ⓓ $\frac{2}{4}$

9. Sheila weaves baskets using reeds. She uses 48 reeds for each basket. How many reeds does she use to weave 3 baskets?

Ⓐ 142

Ⓑ 150

Ⓒ 144

Ⓓ 140

10. Harry has a pottery class from 2:00 P.M to 2:50 P.M. He spends 10 minutes learning how to cut clay and 20 minutes practicing. He spends the rest of the time playing with the clay. How much time does he spend playing with the clay?

Ⓐ 15 minutes

Ⓑ 20 minutes

Ⓒ 25 minutes

Ⓓ 30 minutes

GO ON

11. Which fraction is represented by the sum of these unit fractions?

$$\frac{1}{8} + \frac{1}{8} + \frac{1}{8} + \frac{1}{8} + \frac{1}{8}$$

(A) $\frac{4}{8}$ (B) $\frac{6}{8}$ (C) $\frac{7}{8}$ (D) $\frac{5}{8}$

12. Piper earns $10 every week walking dogs. She has a savings plan in which she saves $2 each week. How much will she save in 8 weeks?

(A) $18 (C) $16

(B) $80 (D) $20

13. Nathan wants to buy 3 shirts. Each shirt costs $8. He has $16 saved and will borrow the rest of the money from his father. Nathan will pay his father back $2 each week. How many weeks will it take to pay back his father?

Record your answer and fill in the bubbles on the grid. Be sure to use the correct place value.

14. Lou's class collected 127 aluminum cans for recycling in the first week of a can drive, 145 in the second week, and 210 in the third week. How many cans did they collect in all?

(A) 482

(B) 272

(C) 455

(D) 582

15. Rachel draws 3 flowers on each of her thank-you notes. If she makes 8 thank-you notes, how many flowers does she draw?

(A) 11 (C) 5

(B) 24 (D) 21

16. Anderson sold 20 flowers. Julia sold 30 flowers. Together, they sold 10 flowers each day. For how many days did they sell flowers?

(A) 5 (C) 3

(B) 2 (D) 10

GO ON

17. Grace has this money in her wallet.

How much money does Grace have?

Ⓐ $1.04   Ⓒ $1.39

Ⓑ $1.25   Ⓓ $1.29

18. Which measurement unit should be used for the liquid volume of the watering can?

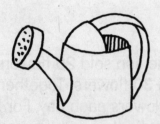

Ⓐ liters

Ⓑ pounds

Ⓒ grams

Ⓓ feet

19. The diagram shows the sketch of the floor of a tree house. Each unit square is 1 square foot.

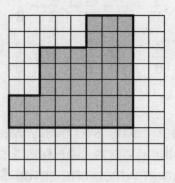

What is the area of the floor of the treehouse?

Record your answer and fill in the bubbles on the grid. Be sure to use the correct place value.

⓪	⓪	⓪	.
①	①	①	
②	②	②	
③	③	③	
④	④	④	
⑤	⑤	⑤	
⑥	⑥	⑥	
⑦	⑦	⑦	
⑧	⑧	⑧	
⑨	⑨	⑨	

20. There were 74 people who came to a play on Friday. There were 28 more people who came to the play on Saturday than on Friday. How many people came to see the play in all?

Ⓐ 102   Ⓒ 176

Ⓑ 156   Ⓓ 166

GO ON →

21. Callie lined up her toy cars in 4 rows. She put 7 cars in each row. How many toy cars does Callie have?

(A) 24   (C) 11

(B) 28   (D) 21

22. Josh has 15 soccer medals. Which describes one array Josh could make using all of his medals?

(A) 9 rows of 6

(B) 5 rows of 10

(C) 3 rows of 4

(D) 5 rows of 3

23. Avery uses 8 pints of lemon juice and 8 pints of water to make lemonade. About how many cups of lemonade does Avery make?

(A) 32   (C) 16

(B) 8   (D) 4

24. Alec cut two shapes out of contruction paper. Then he cut each shape into two equal parts

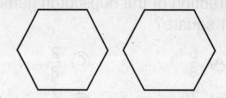

What fraction names each part of one shape?

(A) $\frac{1}{4}$ (C) $\frac{2}{1}$

(B) $\frac{1}{2}$ (D) $\frac{1}{3}$

25. Annabeth has 8 cards. She writes 4 spelling words on each card. How many spelling words does she write?

Record your answer and fill in the bubbles on the grid. Be sure to use the correct place value.

			.	
⓪	⓪	⓪		
①	①	①		
②	②	②		
③	③	③		
④	④	④		
⑤	⑤	⑤		
⑥	⑥	⑥		
⑦	⑦	⑦		
⑧	⑧	⑧		
⑨	⑨	⑨		

GO ON

26. Miguel draws 8 squares on the sidewalk to play hopscotch. Each square is the same size. What fraction of the hopscotch game is 1 square?

Ⓐ $\frac{5}{8}$ Ⓒ $\frac{2}{8}$

Ⓑ $\frac{1}{8}$ Ⓓ $\frac{7}{8}$

27. Theo has 30 pencils. He takes 6 pencils. Then he gives 6 pencils to each of his friends until there are none left. To how many friends does Theo give pencils?

Ⓐ 8

Ⓑ 4

Ⓒ 5

Ⓓ 3

28. Kathleen has 1,208 pennies in a jar. Which digit in 1,208 is in the tens place?

Ⓐ 0

Ⓑ 2

Ⓒ 1

Ⓓ 8

29. Gabriela needs 5 drops of glue for each bow.

Drops of glue	1	2	3	4	5
Bows	5	10	15	20	

How many drops of glue does she need to make 5 bows?

Ⓐ 30   Ⓑ 22   Ⓒ 25   Ⓓ 20

30. Jordan and Melissa had equal-size personal pizzas. Jordan ate $\frac{2}{3}$ of her pizza. Melissa ate $\frac{2}{4}$ of her pizza. Which statement about their pizzas is true?

Jordan   Melissa

Ⓐ Jordan ate more than Melissa because thirds are bigger than fourths.

Ⓑ Jordan and Melissa ate the same amount.

Ⓒ Melissa ate more than Jordan because fourths are bigger than thirds.

Ⓓ There is no way to determine who ate more pizza.

GO ON

31. Lizbeth divided her sandwich into thirds.

Which fraction is equivalent to $\frac{1}{3}$?

Ⓐ $\frac{3}{6}$ Ⓑ $\frac{4}{6}$ Ⓒ $\frac{2}{6}$ Ⓓ $\frac{1}{6}$

32. Elliot has 5 bags. Each bag has 6 tennis balls. How many tennis balls does he have in all?

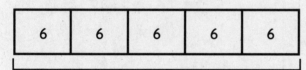

■ tennis balls

Ⓐ 35　　Ⓒ 24

Ⓑ 30　　Ⓓ 25

33. There were 12,408 people that used city buses on Thursday and 15,932 people that used city buses on Saturday. Which statement is correct?

Ⓐ 12,408 = 15,932

Ⓑ 12,408 < 15,932

Ⓒ 12,408 > 15,932

Ⓓ 12,408 + 15,932

34. Sebastian ate $\frac{6}{8}$ of his lunch.

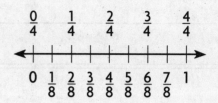

Which fraction is equivalent to $\frac{6}{8}$?

Ⓐ $\frac{3}{4}$

Ⓑ $\frac{1}{4}$

Ⓒ $\frac{4}{4}$

Ⓓ $\frac{2}{4}$

35. Ginny read 108 pages in her book one week and 99 pages the next week. About how many pages did she read in the 2 weeks?

Ⓐ 250

Ⓑ 300

Ⓒ 200

Ⓓ 100

GO ON

36. Twelve friends share 2 bananas equally.

What fraction of a banana does each friend get?

(A) $\frac{1}{2}$ (C) $\frac{1}{6}$

(B) $\frac{1}{4}$ (D) $\frac{1}{8}$

37. Carla found 34 pinecones on a hike. Zoe found 12 fewer pinecones than Carla. How many pinecones did Carla and Zoe find altogether?

Record your answer and fill in the bubbles on the grid. Be sure to use the correct place value.

			.
⓪	⓪	⓪	
①	①	①	
②	②	②	
③	③	③	
④	④	④	
⑤	⑤	⑤	
⑥	⑥	⑥	
⑦	⑦	⑦	
⑧	⑧	⑧	
⑨	⑨	⑨	

38. Jeremy wrote 3 paragraphs. Caleb wrote 2 times as many paragraphs as Jeremy. Which expression represents the number of paragraphs Caleb wrote?

(A) 3×2 (C) $3 + 3 + 3$

(B) $2 + 3$ (D) 4×2

39. Hot dog buns come in packages of 8. How many buns are in 4 packages?

(A) 12 (B) 32 (C) 16 (D) 28

40. Which shape has 3 sides?

(A)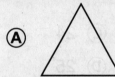

(B)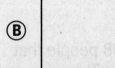

(C)

(D)

GO ON

41. Between which two thousands is 3,110 on the number line?

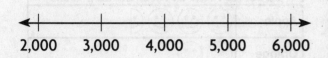

2,000   3,000   4,000   5,000   6,000

(A) 3,000 and 4,000

(B) 2,000 and 3,000

(C) 4,000 and 5,000

(D) 5,000 and 6,000

42. Which shows the numbers ordered from least to greatest?

(A) $616 < 578 < 584$

(B) $578 < 616 < 584$

(C) $616 < 584 < 578$

(D) $578 < 584 < 616$

43. Brittney earns money mowing her grandmother's lawn. Which word describes the money she earns?

(A) saving   (C) income

(B) spending   (D) giving

44. Jason drew these quadrilaterals.

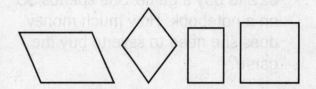

How many rectangles did he draw?

(A) 4   (B) 2   (C) 3   (D) 1

45. Adam has 46 stickers. He puts 10 of them on a sheet of paper. He divides the rest equally among 6 friends. How many stickers does he give each friend?

(A) 5   (C) 6

(B) 7   (D) 4

46. Helena drew a number line.

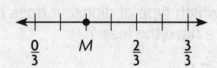

$\frac{0}{3}$ M $\frac{2}{3}$ $\frac{3}{3}$

Which fraction names point M?

(A) $\frac{3}{3}$ (C) $\frac{1}{3}$

(B) $\frac{3}{1}$ (D) $\frac{2}{3}$

GO ON

47. Mara has $12. She wants to save $22 to buy a game. She spends $5 on a notebook. How much money does she need to save to buy the game?

Ⓐ $15

Ⓑ $17

Ⓒ $7

Ⓓ $19

48. A store sells toy dinosaurs. When the store has more of an item, it charges less. The table shows the price for each kind of toy dinosaur.

Toy Dinosaurs	
Dinosaur	Price
T. Rex	$4
Stegosaurus	$5
Velociraptor	$9
Triceratops	$5

Of which type of dinosaur does the store have the least?

Ⓐ T. Rex

Ⓑ Stegosaurus

Ⓒ Velociraptor

Ⓓ Triceratops

Use the pictograph for 49–50.

Favorite Fruit in Mrs. Garza's Class	
Apple	☺ ☺ ☺ ◖
Orange	☺ ☺
Banana	☺ ◖
Grapes	☺ ☺

Each ☺ = 2 students.

49. How many students chose apple or orange?

Ⓐ 11

Ⓑ 4

Ⓒ 7

Ⓓ 10

50. Which fruit did the least number of students choose?

Ⓐ apple

Ⓑ banana

Ⓒ orange

Ⓓ grapes

STOP

Fill in the bubble for the correct answer.

1. Kim used a model to show a number.

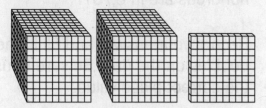

What number did Kim show?

(A) 2,100   (C) 21,000

(B) 21   (D) 210

2. A boulder weighs 1,032 pounds. Which model shows 1,032?

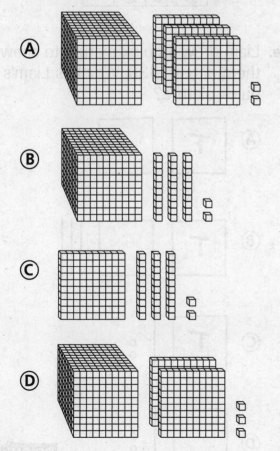

3. A store sells pencils in crates of 1,000, boxes of 100, packets of 10, and single pencils. A school needs 48,392 pencils. Which is a way to buy this exact amount?

(A) 4 crates, 8 boxes, 9 packets, 2 singles

(B) 48 crates, 13 boxes, 9 packets, and 2 singles

(C) 48 crates, 3 boxes, 9 packets, and 2 singles

(D) 4 crates, 18 boxes, 3 packets, and 9 singles

4. A librarian recorded this for the number of books in the library.

$$30,000 + 900 + 80 + 7$$

Which shows the number in standard form?

(A) 3,987

(B) 39,087

(C) 39,870

(D) 30,987

GO ON

5. There were 896 fans at a baseball game.

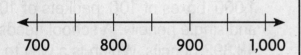

What is this number rounded to the nearest hundred?

(A) 700   (C) 900

(B) 800   (D) 1,000

6. The number of visitors at a zoo was 1,379 on Saturday; 1,463 on Sunday; 1,368 on Monday; and 2,030 on Tuesday. On which day did the **least** number of visitors go to the zoo?

(A) Saturday   (C) Tuesday

(B) Monday   (D) Sunday

7. Which correctly compares the lengths of ribbons that are 8,392 centimeters long and 8,894 centimeters long?

8,392 ⬤ 8,894

(A) <   (C) =

(B) >   (D) +

8. The highest point in Texas is Guadalupe Peak. It is 8,751 feet above sea level. How many hundreds are in 8,751?

Record your answer and fill in the bubbles on the grid. Be sure to use the correct place value.

⓪	⓪	⓪	.
①	①	①	
②	②	②	
③	③	③	
④	④	④	
⑤	⑤	⑤	
⑥	⑥	⑥	
⑦	⑦	⑦	
⑧	⑧	⑧	
⑨	⑨	⑨	

9. Liam drew a quick picture to show the number 1,130. Which is Liam's quick picture?

(A)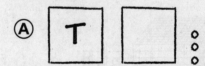

(B)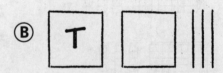

(C)

(D)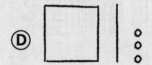

GO ON

10. A factory sells pencils in three kinds of boxes. Large boxes hold 1,000 pencils, medium boxes hold 100 pencils, and small boxes hold 10 pencils. If a school ordered 1 large box, 9 medium boxes, and 8 small boxes, how many pencils did they order?

(A) 1,908

(B) 1,098

(C) 1,980

(D) 198

11. Which point on the number line shows 9,368?

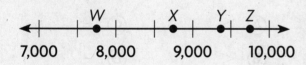

(A) X

(B) Z

(C) Y

(D) W

12. According to a recent census, the population of El Paso was 649,121. Which digit in 649,121 is in the ten thousands place?

(A) 6   (C) 9

(B) 4   (D) 1

13. Kayla has 73 coins in a jar.

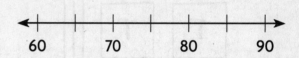

What is this number rounded to the nearest ten?

(A) 70   (C) 90

(B) 60   (D) 80

14. There were 32,865 toys made at a factory last month.

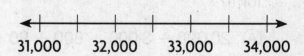

What is this number rounded to the nearest thousand?

(A) 31,000   (C) 33,000

(B) 34,000   (D) 32,000

GO ON

15. Julio's dad drove 1,432 miles on vacation. What is this number rounded to the nearest thousand?

Ⓐ 1,000   Ⓒ 3,000

Ⓑ 2,000   Ⓓ 4,000

16. Ben drew a quick picture of a number.

What number did Ben show?

Ⓐ 23   Ⓒ 2,300

Ⓑ 2,030   Ⓓ 203

17. The distance from Earth to the moon is about 238,900 miles. What is this number in expanded form?

Ⓐ 20,000 + 3,000 + 800 + 90

Ⓑ 200,000 + 30,000 + 8,000 + 900

Ⓒ 200,000 + 3,000 + 800 + 90

Ⓓ 20,000 + 30,000 + 8,000 + 900

18. Students at Jackie's school collected 2,185 cans of corn, 1,169 cans of peas, and 2,147 cans of beans. Which shows these numbers in order from greatest to least?

Ⓐ 2,145; 2,187; 1,169

Ⓑ 2,185; 1,169; 2,145

Ⓒ 2,185; 2,147; 1,169

Ⓓ 1,169; 2,147; 2,185

19. Which correctly compares the two numbers?

56,731 ⬤ 56,713

Ⓐ >   Ⓒ =

Ⓑ <   Ⓓ −

20. About 36,250 people ride the light rail in Houston each day. How many ten thousands are in 36,250?

Ⓐ 36   Ⓒ 5

Ⓑ 6   Ⓓ 3

STOP

Fill in the bubble for the correct answer.

1. Meg cut a triangle into 2 equal parts. She shaded 1 part.

What fraction names the shaded part of Meg's triangle?

Ⓐ $\frac{1}{3}$ 　　Ⓒ $\frac{2}{1}$

Ⓑ $\frac{2}{2}$ 　　Ⓓ $\frac{1}{2}$

2. Caleb cut a circle into 6 equal parts. He took away 2 parts.

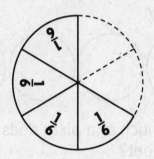

What fraction of the circle is left?

Ⓐ $\frac{1}{6}$ 　　Ⓒ $\frac{4}{6}$

Ⓑ $\frac{2}{6}$ 　　Ⓓ $\frac{5}{6}$

3. Elle drew a number line.

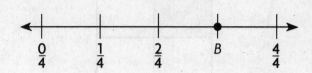

Which fraction names point *B*?

Ⓐ $\frac{2}{4}$ 　　Ⓒ $\frac{4}{4}$

Ⓑ $\frac{3}{4}$ 　　Ⓓ $\frac{5}{4}$

4. What fraction is represented by the sum of $\frac{1}{8} + \frac{1}{8} + \frac{1}{8}$?

Ⓐ $\frac{1}{8}$ 　　Ⓒ $\frac{3}{8}$

Ⓑ $\frac{2}{8}$ 　　Ⓓ $\frac{4}{8}$

5. Lin ate $\frac{3}{4}$ of a sandwich. Which shows $\frac{3}{4}$ written as a sum of unit fractions?

Ⓐ $\frac{3}{4} + \frac{3}{4}$ 　　Ⓒ $\frac{1}{4} + \frac{1}{4} + \frac{1}{4}$

Ⓑ $\frac{1}{4} + \frac{2}{4}$ 　　Ⓓ $\frac{1}{4} + \frac{1}{4}$

GO ON ➡

6. Connor shaded part of a square.

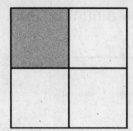

Which fraction names the shaded part?

(A) $\frac{1}{4}$ (C) $\frac{4}{4}$

(B) $\frac{2}{4}$ (D) $\frac{3}{4}$

7. Four friends bought 2 muffins.

They divided the muffins equally. How much of a muffin did each friend get?

(A) 1 fourth

(B) 4 halves

(C) 4 fourths

(D) 1 half

8. Aidan colors part of a circle.

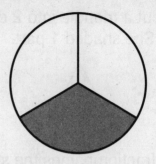

Which fraction names the shaded part?

(A) $\frac{1}{3}$ (C) $\frac{3}{3}$

(B) $\frac{2}{3}$ (D) $\frac{4}{3}$

9. Eight friends share 4 small pizzas equally.

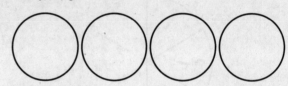

How much of a pizza does each friend get?

(A) $\frac{1}{2}$

(B) $\frac{1}{4}$

(C) $\frac{1}{8}$

(D) $\frac{1}{6}$

GO ON

10. Missy divides a pie into 8 equal parts. What fraction names one part of the pie?

(A) $\frac{1}{8}$ (C) $\frac{8}{1}$

(B) $\frac{2}{8}$ (D) $\frac{8}{8}$

11. Sheila has a fraction strip.

$\frac{1}{3}$	$\frac{1}{3}$	$\frac{1}{3}$

She wants to shade the fraction strip to show $\frac{2}{3}$. How many parts of the fraction strip should Sheila shade?

Record your answer and fill in the bubbles on the grid. Be sure to use the correct place value.

⓪	⓪	⓪	.
①	①	①	
②	②	②	
③	③	③	
④	④	④	
⑤	⑤	⑤	
⑥	⑥	⑥	
⑦	⑦	⑦	
⑧	⑧	⑧	
⑨	⑨	⑨	

12. Diego shaded the fraction strip to show the part of an hour that he practiced piano.

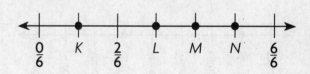

What fraction of an hour did Diego practice?

(A) $\frac{1}{4}$ (B) $\frac{2}{4}$ (C) $\frac{3}{4}$ (D) $\frac{4}{4}$

13. Talia made a number line.

$$\overset{\begin{matrix} & K & & L & M & N & \\ \frac{0}{6} & & \frac{2}{6} & & & & \frac{6}{6} \end{matrix}}{\longleftrightarrow}$$

Which point represents $\frac{5}{6}$?

(A) K   (B) L   (C) M   (D) N

14. What fraction of the clock is **NOT** shaded?

(A) $\frac{1}{4}$ (B) $\frac{2}{4}$ (C) $\frac{3}{4}$ (D) $\frac{4}{4}$

GO ON

15. Twelve friends share 2 peaches equally.

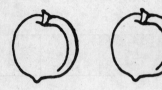

What fraction of a peach does each friend get?

Ⓐ $\frac{1}{6}$ Ⓑ $\frac{2}{6}$ Ⓒ $\frac{3}{6}$ Ⓓ $\frac{4}{6}$

16. Austin made a number line.

Which fraction names point *G*?

Ⓐ $\frac{1}{8}$ Ⓑ $\frac{3}{8}$ Ⓒ $\frac{5}{8}$ Ⓓ $\frac{6}{8}$

17. Carla walked $\frac{5}{6}$ of a mile. How many parts of this fraction strip should she shade to show $\frac{5}{6}$?

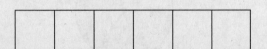

Ⓐ 3   Ⓑ 4   Ⓒ 5   Ⓓ 6

18. Six friends share 2 bananas equally.

What fraction of a banana does each friend get?

Ⓐ $\frac{1}{3}$ Ⓑ $\frac{2}{3}$ Ⓒ $\frac{3}{3}$ Ⓓ $\frac{4}{3}$

19. Molly divided a pie into 8 equal pieces. She ate 1 piece.

What fraction of the pie did Molly eat?

Ⓐ $\frac{8}{1}$ Ⓑ $\frac{1}{8}$ Ⓒ $\frac{2}{8}$ Ⓓ $\frac{8}{8}$

20. Pete drew a number line.

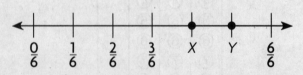

Which fraction names point *X*?

Ⓐ $\frac{6}{1}$ Ⓑ $\frac{5}{6}$ Ⓒ $\frac{4}{6}$ Ⓓ $\frac{3}{6}$

Fill in the bubble for the correct answer.

1. Evan practiced piano for $\frac{1}{2}$ hour.

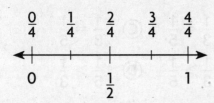

   Which fraction is equivalent to $\frac{1}{2}$?

   Ⓐ $\frac{1}{4}$ Ⓑ $\frac{2}{4}$ Ⓒ $\frac{3}{4}$ Ⓓ $\frac{4}{4}$

2. Ginny's vase weighs $\frac{5}{6}$ pound. Alex's vase weighs $\frac{3}{6}$ pound. Which comparison is correct?

   Ⓐ $\frac{5}{6} > \frac{3}{6}$ Ⓒ $\frac{5}{6} = \frac{3}{6}$

   Ⓑ $\frac{5}{6} < \frac{3}{6}$ Ⓓ $\frac{3}{6} > \frac{5}{6}$

3. Carlo walks $\frac{5}{8}$ of a mile. How many parts of this fraction strip should he shade to show $\frac{5}{8}$?

$\frac{1}{8}$	$\frac{1}{8}$	$\frac{1}{8}$	$\frac{1}{8}$	$\frac{1}{8}$	$\frac{1}{8}$	$\frac{1}{8}$	$\frac{1}{8}$

   Ⓐ 3   Ⓑ 4   Ⓒ 5   Ⓓ 8

4. Seth and Karsten had equal-size apples. Seth ate $\frac{5}{8}$ of his apple. Karsten ate $\frac{5}{6}$ of his apple. Which statement about their apples is true?

   Ⓐ Seth ate more than Karsten.

   Ⓑ Seth and Karsten ate the same amount.

   Ⓒ Karsten ate more than Seth.

   Ⓓ There is no way to tell who ate more apple.

5. Calvin served $\frac{2}{8}$ of an apple pie to his guests. He served an equivalent fraction of cherry pie of the same size.

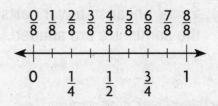

   Which fraction is equivalent to $\frac{2}{8}$?

   Ⓐ $\frac{1}{2}$ Ⓑ $\frac{1}{4}$ Ⓒ $\frac{2}{4}$ Ⓓ $\frac{3}{4}$

GO ON

6. Helen shaded $\frac{2}{4}$ of one sheet of paper and $\frac{3}{4}$ of another sheet of paper.

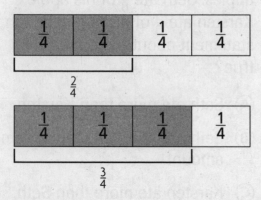

$\frac{2}{4}$

$\frac{3}{4}$

If the sheets are the same size, which statement is true?

(A) It is not possible to compare the two fractions.

(B) $\frac{2}{4} > \frac{3}{4}$ because halves are greater than thirds.

(C) $\frac{2}{4} = \frac{3}{4}$ because the denominators are the same.

(D) $\frac{2}{4} < \frac{3}{4}$ because fewer parts of the same size are shaded.

7. Blake waited for a bus for $\frac{2}{3}$ hour.

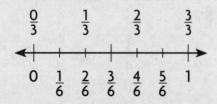

Which fraction is equivalent to $\frac{2}{3}$?

(A) $\frac{2}{6}$ (B) $\frac{3}{6}$ (C) $\frac{4}{6}$ (D) $\frac{5}{6}$

8. Celia read $\frac{1}{3}$ of a book. Micah read $\frac{1}{5}$ of the same book. Which statement is true?

(A) $\frac{1}{3} < \frac{1}{5}$ (C) $\frac{1}{3} = \frac{1}{5}$

(B) $\frac{1}{3} > \frac{1}{5}$ (D) $\frac{1}{5} > \frac{1}{3}$

9. Maya shaded $\frac{4}{6}$ of a rectangle.

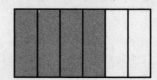

How many thirds of the rectangle did she shade?

Record your answer and fill in the bubbles on the grid. Be sure to use the correct place value.

⓪	⓪	⓪	.
①	①	①	
②	②	②	
③	③	③	
④	④	④	
⑤	⑤	⑤	
⑥	⑥	⑥	
⑦	⑦	⑦	
⑧	⑧	⑧	
⑨	⑨	⑨	

GO ON

10. Ada read $\frac{1}{2}$ of a book.

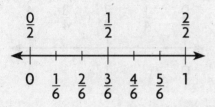

Which fraction is equivalent to $\frac{1}{2}$?

(A) $\frac{2}{6}$ (B) $\frac{3}{6}$ (C) $\frac{4}{6}$ (D) $\frac{6}{6}$

11. Karl shaded Circle A. He wants to shade Circle B to show an equivalent fraction.

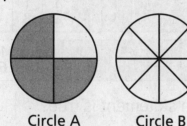

Circle A   Circle B

What fraction of Circle B should Karl shade?

(A) $\frac{6}{8}$ (B) $\frac{2}{3}$ (C) $\frac{5}{6}$ (D) $\frac{4}{8}$

12. What fraction of the pizza has pepperoni?

(A) $\frac{1}{8}$ (B) $\frac{5}{8}$ (C) $\frac{6}{8}$ (D) $\frac{8}{8}$

13. Devin drew a number line.

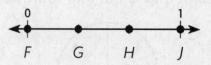

Which point represents $\frac{3}{3}$?

(A) F   (B) G   (C) H   (D) J

14. Dana painted $\frac{4}{6}$ of a plate in art class. Ben painted $\frac{4}{8}$ of a plate.

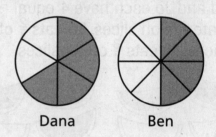

Dana   Ben

If the plates are the same size, which is true?

(A) $\frac{4}{6} > \frac{4}{8}$ because sixths are larger than eighths.

(B) $\frac{4}{6} = \frac{4}{8}$ because the numerators are the same.

(C) $\frac{4}{6} < \frac{4}{8}$ because eighths are larger than sixths.

(D) $\frac{4}{6} > \frac{4}{8}$ because sixths are smaller than eighths.

GO ON

15. Kate and Brad equally share a peach that is cut into fourths.

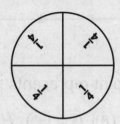

How much of the peach does each student get?

Ⓐ $\frac{1}{4}$ Ⓑ $\frac{2}{4}$ Ⓒ $\frac{3}{4}$ Ⓓ $\frac{4}{4}$

16. Ed and Jo each have 4 equal watermelon slices. Ed eats $\frac{2}{4}$ of his slices. Jo eats $\frac{3}{4}$ of her slices.

Ed   Jo

Which statement is true?

Ⓐ $\frac{2}{4} < \frac{3}{4}$ Ⓒ $\frac{3}{4} < \frac{2}{4}$

Ⓑ $\frac{3}{4} = \frac{2}{4}$ Ⓓ $\frac{2}{4} > \frac{3}{4}$

17. Lin shaded $\frac{2}{3}$ of a circle.

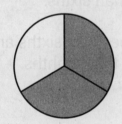

Which fraction is equivalent to $\frac{2}{3}$?

Ⓐ $\frac{2}{6}$ Ⓑ $\frac{3}{6}$ Ⓒ $\frac{4}{6}$ Ⓓ $\frac{5}{6}$

18. Nicholas biked $\frac{2}{4}$ mile.

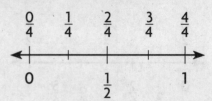

Which fraction is equivalent to $\frac{2}{4}$?

Ⓐ $\frac{1}{2}$ Ⓑ $\frac{1}{3}$ Ⓒ $\frac{2}{2}$ Ⓓ $\frac{2}{3}$

19. Jesse ate $\frac{5}{8}$ of a sandwich. Meg ate $\frac{5}{6}$ of an equal-size sandwich.

$\frac{1}{8}$	$\frac{1}{8}$	$\frac{1}{8}$	$\frac{1}{8}$	$\frac{1}{8}$	$\frac{1}{8}$	$\frac{1}{8}$	$\frac{1}{8}$

$\frac{1}{6}$	$\frac{1}{6}$	$\frac{1}{6}$	$\frac{1}{6}$	$\frac{1}{6}$	$\frac{1}{6}$

Which statement is true?

Ⓐ $\frac{5}{8} > \frac{5}{6}$ Ⓒ $\frac{5}{6} < \frac{5}{8}$

Ⓑ $\frac{5}{8} = \frac{5}{6}$ Ⓓ $\frac{5}{6} > \frac{5}{8}$

20. Mia has $\frac{6}{6}$ of an orange.

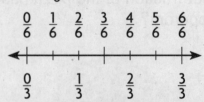

Which fraction is equivalent to $\frac{6}{6}$?

Ⓐ $\frac{3}{3}$ Ⓑ $\frac{2}{3}$ Ⓒ $\frac{1}{3}$ Ⓓ $\frac{1}{6}$

STOP

Fill in the bubble for the correct answer.

1. Aisha used 128 large paper clips and 285 small paper clips for a project. Which is the best estimate of the total number of paper clips she used?

Ⓐ 100

Ⓑ 300

Ⓒ 400

Ⓓ 200

100
+ 300
400

2. Colin has this money in his wallet.

How much money does Colin have in his wallet?

Ⓐ $2.78

Ⓒ $6.87

Ⓑ $6.78

Ⓓ $6.88

3. Maya has 72 stamps in her collection. Jake has 41 stamps. Which is the best estimate for the total number of stamps?

Ⓐ 110

Ⓒ 120

Ⓑ 150

Ⓓ 130

4. There are 138 third graders and 157 fourth graders at Linwood Elementary School. How many third and fourth graders are there altogether?

Ⓐ 295

Ⓒ 285

Ⓑ 294

Ⓓ 281

5. A farmer sold 48 tomatoes and 24 cucumbers at a market. Round each number to the nearest ten to estimate the sum. About how many tomatoes and cucumbers did the farmer sell in all?

Ⓐ 80

Ⓒ 30

Ⓑ 70

Ⓓ 60

GO ON

6. On a bike trip, Cara biked 21 miles the first day, 34 miles the second day, and 27 miles the third day. How many miles did she bike the three days?

Record your answer and fill in the bubbles on the grid. Be sure to use the correct place value.

⓪	⓪	⓪	.
①	①	①	
②	②	②	
③	③	③	
④	④	④	
⑤	⑤	⑤	
⑥	⑥	⑥	
⑦	⑦	⑦	
⑧	⑧	⑧	
⑨	⑨	⑨	

7. Taylor scored 334 points in her first word game. She scored 285 in her second game. What is the total number of points Taylor scored?

Ⓐ 519

Ⓑ 529

Ⓒ 619

Ⓓ 629

8. There are 38 roses, 35 tulips, and 22 lilies. The Commutative Property of Addition can help you add. Which shows the Commutative Property of Addition?

Ⓐ $38 + 35 + 22 = (38 + 35) + 22$

Ⓑ $38 + 35 + 22 = 38 + (35 + 22)$

Ⓒ $38 + 35 + 22 = 38 + 22 + 35$

Ⓓ $38 + 35 + 22 = (38 + 35 + 22)$

9. Aliyah spent 47 minutes playing soccer on Saturday. She spent 32 minutes playing soccer on Sunday. Which is the best estimate for the total number of minutes she played soccer on these two days?

Ⓐ 80 minutes

Ⓑ 90 minutes

Ⓒ 70 minutes

Ⓓ 60 minutes

10. Sophie's family packed for a trip. Their suitcases weigh 45, 45, and 53 pounds. What is the total weight of their suitcases?

Ⓐ 98 pounds   Ⓒ 143 pounds

Ⓑ 140 pounds   Ⓓ 145 pounds

11. Ethan used 272 short craft sticks and 326 long craft sticks to build a boat. Which shows the best compatible numbers to estimate the total number of sticks?

(A) 200 + 300

(B) 275 + 325

(C) 300 + 400

(D) 250 + 300

12. Mayim collected 128 shells on the beach on Friday. She collected 179 shells on Saturday and 103 shells on Sunday. Which is the best estimate for the total number of shells Mayim collected?

(A) 100

(B) 200

(C) 300

(D) 400

13. Jonah used building bricks for a project. He used 318 red bricks. He used 20 more blue bricks than red bricks. How many red and blue bricks did Jonah use?

(A) 338

(B) 646

(C) 656

(D) 636

14. Jackson glued 87 blue petals and 105 yellow petals onto paper flowers to make party decorations. Which is the best estimate for the total number of petals he glued?

(A) 250   (C) 200

(B) 100   (D) 300

15. Last week, Elena spent 118 minutes practicing piano, 164 minutes practicing violin, and 102 minutes practicing cello. How many minutes did she practice in all?

(A) 374 minutes

(B) 384 minutes

(C) 474 minutes

(D) 484 minutes

GO ON

16. Olga has exactly $12.55. She has one $10 bill, two $1 bills, and 10 coins. Which coins could Olga have?

Ⓐ 5 dimes, 5 pennies

Ⓑ 5 quarters, 5 pennies

Ⓒ 2 quarters, 5 nickels, 3 pennies

Ⓓ 2 dimes, 8 nickels

17. Elizabeth needs one rope that is 188 inches long for a project. She needs another rope that is 523 inches long. Which is the best estimate for the total length of the two ropes?

Ⓐ 500 inches

Ⓑ 600 inches

Ⓒ 700 inches

Ⓓ 800 inches

18. Marty and Sara collected tickets for a school play. On the first night, they collected 287 tickets. On the second night, they collected 127 tickets. How many total tickets did they take on both nights?

Ⓐ 314   Ⓒ 404

Ⓑ 394   Ⓓ 414

19. The distance from Mari's house to her school is 480 feet. How many feet does Mari walk when she walks to and from school?

Ⓐ 880 feet

Ⓑ 580 feet

Ⓒ 860 feet

Ⓓ 960 feet

20. A bakery delivered 248 loaves of bread on Tuesday and 354 loaves of bread on Wednesday. How many loaves of bread did the bakery deliver in all on Tuesday and Wednesday?

Ⓐ 692   Ⓒ 592

Ⓑ 602   Ⓓ 502

Fill in the bubble for the correct answer.

1. Jonathan read 272 pages on Sunday. This was 114 more pages than he read on Saturday. How many pages did Jonathan read on Saturday?

   (A) 44

   (B) 52

   (C) 262

   (D) 158

2. Jen collects 225 pennies. Kyle collects 247 pennies

225	247

   ▪ pennies

   How many pennies do Jen and Kyle collect in all?

   (A) 22

   (B) 472

   (C) 32

   (D) 462

3. Cara scored 480 points in a word game. Devin scored 105 more points than Cara. Ellie scored 250 fewer points than Devin. How many points did Ellie score?

   (A) 835   (C) 585

   (B) 335   (D) 230

4. Sadie has 81 stamps of famous people and 58 stamps of famous places. Which is the best estimate of how many more stamps of famous peope Sadie has than stamps of famous places?

   (A) 20   (B) 30   (C) 50   (D) 40

5. Tate's family drove 283 miles on Saturday and 104 miles on Sunday. Which is the best estimate of how many more miles they drove on Saturday than on Sunday?

   (A) 400   (C) 100

   (B) 200   (D) 300

GO ON ➡

6. There are 337 girls at Edgewood Elementary. There are 148 more boys than girls. How many girls and boys are students at Edgewood Elementary?

- Ⓐ 189
- Ⓒ 485
- Ⓑ 526
- Ⓓ 822

7. There are 653 yellow marbles at a toy store. There are 152 fewer green marbles. How many green marbles are there?

- Ⓐ 805
- Ⓒ 705
- Ⓑ 501
- Ⓓ 815

8. There are 418 students at a school. Of these, 327 ride the bus home. How many of the students do **NOT** ride the bus home?

- Ⓐ 91
- Ⓒ 735
- Ⓑ 191
- Ⓓ 74

9. There are 374 buses in Maya's city. There are 207 taxis. Which is the best estimate of how many more buses than taxis there are in Maya's city?

- Ⓐ 75
- Ⓑ 175
- Ⓒ 225
- Ⓓ 37

10. There are 228 red raffle tickets at a school fair. There are 304 blue raffle tickets. There are 127 fewer green raffle tickets than red and blue raffle tickets together. How many green raffle tickets are there?

- Ⓐ 405
- Ⓑ 355
- Ⓒ 659
- Ⓓ 425

GO ON

11. Cari did 67 push-ups in gym class. Brent did 18 fewer push-ups than Cari. How many push-ups did Brent do?

Record your answer and fill in the bubbles on the grid. Be sure to use the correct place value.

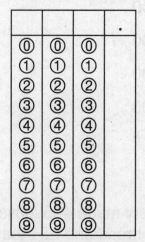

12. Marcus collects 34 pebbles on a hike. Josie collects 13 fewer pebbles than Marcus.

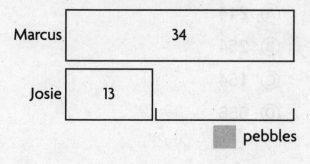

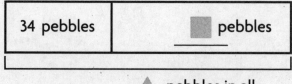

How many pebbles did they collect in all?

Ⓐ 47   Ⓑ 55   Ⓒ 65   Ⓓ 21

13. Of the 497 students and parents at a school open house, 339 were students. Which is the best estimate of the number of parents at the open house?

Ⓐ 800   Ⓒ 200

Ⓑ 300   Ⓓ 100

14. There are 228 blue cars and 189 black cars at a car dealership. There are 121 fewer white cars than blue and black cars together. How many white cars are there?

Ⓐ 417   Ⓒ 296

Ⓑ 306   Ⓓ 538

15. A plane flies from New York to Dallas with 382 passengers. In Dallas, 177 passengers get off the plane. How many passengers stay on the plane?

Ⓐ 205

Ⓑ 115

Ⓒ 215

Ⓓ 559

GO ON

16. Tyler travels 429 miles to summer camp. Liza travels 136 miles to summer camp. How many more miles does Tyler travel than Liza?

Ⓐ 303

Ⓒ 213

Ⓑ 293

Ⓓ 565

17. At a baseball game, Lia sold 67 boxes of popcorn. Marius sold 58. Which is the best estimate of how many more boxes of popcorn Lia sold than Marius?

Ⓐ 10

Ⓒ 120

Ⓑ 30

Ⓓ 20

18. Camden and Rajeev each have 137 coins. Eli has 53 fewer coins than Camden and Rajeev have together. How many coins does Eli have?

Ⓐ 84

Ⓒ 190

Ⓑ 221

Ⓓ 274

19. There were 571 people at a swimming pool on Sunday. There were 396 people at the same pool on Saturday. Which is the best estimate of how many more people were at the pool on Sunday than on Saturday?

Ⓐ 200

Ⓑ 500

Ⓒ 300

Ⓓ 400

20. A bakery made 405 loaves of wheat bread and 251 loaves of white bread. How many more loaves of wheat bread than white bread did the bakery make?

Ⓐ 244

Ⓑ 254

Ⓒ 154

Ⓓ 656

STOP

Fill in the bubble for the correct answer.

1. Carlos completed $\frac{5}{8}$ of the tests for his martial arts class. Which shows $\frac{5}{8}$ written as a sum of unit fractions?

   (A) $\frac{1}{8} + \frac{1}{8} + \frac{1}{8} + \frac{1}{8} + \frac{1}{8}$

   (B) $\frac{2}{8} + \frac{3}{8}$

   (C) $\frac{5}{8} + \frac{5}{8}$

   (D) $\frac{1}{4} + \frac{3}{8}$

2. Laney has the money shown. How much money does Laney have?

   (A) $13.55   (C) $13.42

   (B) $13.67   (D) $13.57

3. Albert biked 18 miles on Monday. This was 12 fewer miles than he biked on Sunday. How many miles did he bike on Sunday?

   (A) 6   (B) 20   (C) 30   (D) 32

4. A music collector has 2,253 classical songs, 2,025 country songs, and 2,513 bluegrass songs in her collection. Which shows the numbers of songs in order from least to greatest?

   (A) 2,025; 2513; 2,253

   (B) 2,025; 2,253; 2,513

   (C) 2,253; 2513; 2,025

   (D) 2,513; 2,253; 2,025

5. Mia has finished $\frac{2}{5}$ of her homework. Samuel has finished $\frac{2}{6}$ of his homework. Which statement is true?

   (A) $\frac{2}{6} = \frac{2}{5}$ (C) $\frac{2}{5} < \frac{2}{6}$

   (B) $\frac{2}{6} > \frac{2}{5}$ (D) $\frac{2}{5} > \frac{2}{6}$

GO ON

6. Six friends share 3 small pizzas equally.

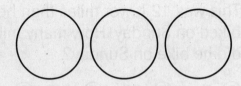

How much of a pizza does each friend get?

(A) $\frac{1}{9}$ (B) $\frac{1}{3}$ (C) $\frac{1}{2}$ (D) $\frac{1}{6}$

7. Chris used 155 small building blocks and 398 large building blocks to build a tower. Which shows compatible numbers he should use to estimate the total number of blocks?

(A) 200 + 300

(B) 150 + 400

(C) 150 + 375

(D) 125 + 425

8. The retractable roof of Cowboys Stadium is approximately 660,802 square feet. Which digit in 660,802 is in the hundreds place?

(A) 0   (B) 8   (C) 6   (D) 2

9. There are 288 adult African elephants and 156 young African elephants in a nature preserve. How many African elephants are in the nature preserve?

(A) 444   (C) 334

(B) 344   (D) 434

10. Luke ran $\frac{3}{4}$ of a mile.

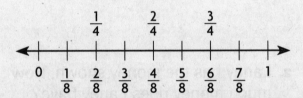

Which fraction is equivalent to $\frac{3}{4}$?

(A) $\frac{3}{8}$ (C) $\frac{6}{8}$

(B) $\frac{4}{8}$ (D) $\frac{1}{8}$

11. Gabriel has 62 red grapes and 34 green grapes. Which is the best estimate of how many more red grapes he has than green grapes?

(A) 110   (B) 20   (C) 30   (D) 90

GO ON

12. Jenna drew a circle and divided it into 3 equal parts. She colored 2 of the parts blue.

What fraction of the circle did she color?

Ⓐ $\frac{1}{3}$ Ⓑ $\frac{2}{3}$ Ⓒ $\frac{3}{4}$ Ⓓ $\frac{1}{2}$

13. Olivia used tiles to make a pattern. She used 28 square tiles. She used 13 more round tiles than square tiles. How many square and round tiles did Olivia use?

Record your answer and fill in the bubbles on the grid. Be sure to use the correct place value.

⓪	⓪	⓪	.
①	①	①	
②	②	②	
③	③	③	
④	④	④	
⑤	⑤	⑤	
⑥	⑥	⑥	
⑦	⑦	⑦	
⑧	⑧	⑧	
⑨	⑨	⑨	

14. Students in the Spirit Club sell t-shirts. They order the shirts in boxes of 1,000, 100, 10, or as single t-shirts. They need 3,482 shirts. How can they order this exact amount?

Ⓐ 3 boxes of 1,000; 4 boxes of 100; 8 boxes of 10; 2 singles

Ⓑ 3 boxes of 1,000; 8 boxes of 100; 4 boxes of 10; 2 singles

Ⓒ 2 boxes of 1,000; 4 boxes of 100; 8 boxes of 10; 3 singles

Ⓓ 2 boxes of 1,000; 8 boxes of 100; 4 boxes of 10; 3 singles

15. Ellie has 3 puppies. Their weights are 38, 33, and 36 pounds. What is the total weight of the puppies?

Ⓐ 107 pounds

Ⓑ 114 pounds

Ⓒ 71 pounds

Ⓓ 97 pounds

GO ON

16. The shaded part represents the part of the pie that Eliza served to her friends. What fraction of the pie did she serve?

Ⓐ $\frac{7}{8}$ Ⓒ $\frac{2}{8}$

Ⓑ $\frac{6}{8}$ Ⓓ $\frac{5}{8}$

17. Between which two thousands is 5,389 on the number line?

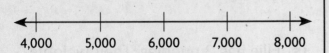

Ⓐ 7,000 and 8,000

Ⓑ 4,000 and 5,000

Ⓒ 6,000 and 7,000

Ⓓ 5,000 and 6,000

18. Jeremiah divides a piece of paper into 4 equal parts. What fraction names one part?

Ⓐ $\frac{1}{4}$ Ⓑ $\frac{3}{4}$ Ⓒ $\frac{4}{4}$ Ⓓ $\frac{4}{1}$

19. Joe spent 33 minutes practicing piano and 28 minutes practicing guitar. Which is the best estimate of the total number of minutes he spent practicing?

Ⓐ 80 minutes   Ⓒ 50 minutes

Ⓑ 70 minutes   Ⓓ 60 minutes

20. Tina and Lane each have an apple divided into sixths. Tina eats $\frac{3}{6}$ of hers and Lane eats $\frac{4}{6}$ of his. Which statement is true?

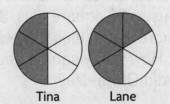

Tina   Lane

Ⓐ $\frac{3}{6} < \frac{4}{6}$ Ⓒ $\frac{4}{6} < \frac{3}{6}$

Ⓑ $\frac{4}{6} = \frac{3}{6}$ Ⓓ $\frac{3}{6} > \frac{4}{6}$

21. Out of the 587 cows on a dairy farm, 119 are calves. Which is the best estimate of the number of adult cows on the dairy farm?

Ⓐ 400

Ⓑ 700

Ⓒ 500

Ⓓ 300

GO ON →

22. The weight of a dolphin at a zoo is 1,157 pounds. Which model shows 1,157?

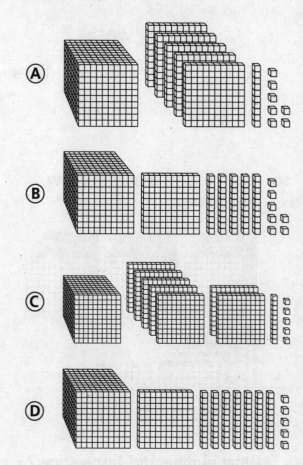

Ⓐ

Ⓑ

Ⓒ

Ⓓ

23. Janine made a number line.

Which point represents $\frac{3}{4}$?

Ⓐ P   Ⓒ Q

Ⓑ R   Ⓓ S

24. Tyler walked $\frac{2}{3}$ of a mile.

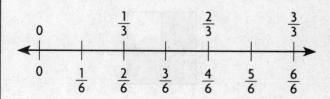

Which fraction is equivalent to $\frac{2}{3}$?

Ⓐ $\frac{3}{6}$ Ⓒ $\frac{1}{6}$

Ⓑ $\frac{2}{6}$ Ⓓ $\frac{4}{6}$

25. Marisol read for 55 minutes on Friday. This was 37 more minutes than she read on Thursday. How many minutes did she read on Thursday?

Record your answer and fill in the bubbles on the grid. Be sure to use the correct place value.

⓪	⓪	⓪	.
①	①	①	
②	②	②	
③	③	③	
④	④	④	
⑤	⑤	⑤	
⑥	⑥	⑥	
⑦	⑦	⑦	
⑧	⑧	⑧	
⑨	⑨	⑨	

GO ON

26. Austin colors $\frac{3}{4}$ of a square.

How many eighths of the square did he color?

(A) $\frac{6}{8}$

(C) $\frac{5}{8}$

(B) $\frac{3}{8}$

(D) $\frac{8}{8}$

27. Darla has 267 animal stickers, 541 sports stickers, and 119 flower stickers. Which is the best estimate of the total number of stickers Darla has?

(A) 700

(C) 1000

(B) 900

(D) 800

28. Maren's apple weighs $\frac{4}{6}$ pound. Ryan's apple weighs $\frac{1}{6}$ pound. Which statement is correct?

(A) $\frac{1}{6} > \frac{4}{6}$

(C) $\frac{4}{6} < \frac{1}{6}$

(B) $\frac{4}{6} = \frac{1}{6}$

(D) $\frac{1}{6} < \frac{4}{6}$

29. Which correctly compares the lengths of sidewalks that are 4,087 feet long and 4,054 feet long?

4,087 ■ 4,054

(A) <   (B) >   (C) =   (D) +

30. Jason used a model to show a number.

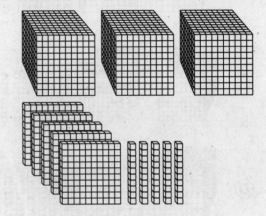

What number did Jason show?

(A) 3,550

(C) 3,505

(B) 3,050

(D) 3,500

STOP

Fill in the bubble for the correct answer.

1. Julia places her stickers in 4 rows. There are 8 stickers in each row. How many stickers does she have in all?

   Ⓐ 12 Ⓑ 28 Ⓒ 24 Ⓓ 32

2. Toby has 5 groups of coins. Each group has 9 coins. Five of Toby's coins are quarters and the rest are pennies. How many pennies does Toby have?

   Ⓐ 19 Ⓑ 20 Ⓒ 40 Ⓓ 45

3. Connor and his mother baked muffins for a school fair. They baked 8 blueberry muffins, 8 strawberry muffins, 8 lemon muffins, and 8 chocolate muffins. Which multiplication sentence shows how many muffins they baked?

   Ⓐ $1 \times 4 = 4$ Ⓒ $2 \times 8 = 16$
   Ⓑ $4 \times 8 = 32$ Ⓓ $1 \times 8 = 8$

4. Greta has 3 pitchers of lemonade for a picnic. Each pitcher has 5 cups of lemonade.

   How many cups of lemonade are there in all?

   Ⓐ 10
   Ⓑ 8
   Ⓒ 5
   Ⓓ 15

5. Libby arranges 18 photos on a poster in 3 rows of 6 photos each. Which is another way she could arrange the 18 photos?

   Ⓐ 2 rows of 9
   Ⓑ 3 rows of 9
   Ⓒ 2 rows of 6
   Ⓓ 6 rows of 4

GO ON

6. Each bag holds 6 apples. Charla buys 1 bag of apples. How many apples does she buy?

Ⓐ 1   Ⓑ 7   Ⓒ 6   Ⓓ 5

7. Oliver has 3 boxes of blocks. Each box has 9 blocks in it. Oliver says the number of blocks is equal to $9 + 9 + 9$. Which is another way to find the number of blocks?

Ⓐ 3×9 Ⓒ 9×9

Ⓑ 1×9 Ⓓ 3×3

8. Delia has 2 rows of shoes. There are 6 shoes in each row. One way to find the number of shoes is to multiply 2×6. Which is another way to find the number of shoes?

Ⓐ Add $2 + 6$.

Ⓑ Add $2 + 2$.

Ⓒ Multiply 6×2.

Ⓓ Multiply 3×6.

9. Emme has 4 tomato plants. Each plant has 4 tomatoes.

0 1 2 3 4 5 6 7 8 9 10 11 12 13 14 15 16 17 18 19 20

How many tomatoes are on the plants?

Ⓐ 4   Ⓒ 12

Ⓑ 8   Ⓓ 16

10. Lily has 3 bags. Each bag has 8 marbles. Three of Lily's marbles are red and the rest are green.

How many green marbles does Lily have?

Record your answer and fill in the bubbles on the grid. Be sure to use the correct place value.

⓪	⓪	⓪	.
①	①	①	
②	②	②	
③	③	③	
④	④	④	
⑤	⑤	⑤	
⑥	⑥	⑥	
⑦	⑦	⑦	
⑧	⑧	⑧	
⑨	⑨	⑨	

GO ON

11. Nolan has 2 boxes of flashcards. Each box has 8 flashcards.

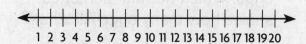

1 2 3 4 5 6 7 8 9 10 11 12 13 14 15 16 17 18 19 20

How many flashcards does Nolan have in all?

Ⓐ 16   Ⓑ 4   Ⓒ 8   Ⓓ 10

12. The students in an after school program place their backpacks in 3 bins. Each bin holds 7 backpacks.

| 7 | 7 | 7 |

 backpacks

How many backpacks can the bins hold?

Ⓐ 10   Ⓑ 21   Ⓒ 24   Ⓓ 4

13. Carla has 12 apples. She arranges them in 4 rows with 3 in each row.

Which is another way she could arrange the 12 apples?

Ⓐ 3 rows of 4   Ⓒ 3 rows of 6

Ⓑ 4 rows of 5   Ⓓ 5 rows of 3

14. Jill sets up 6 rows of chairs with 5 chairs in each row. Cameron sets up 5 rows of chairs with 6 chairs in each row. How many chairs do Jill and Cameron set up in all?

Ⓐ 30   Ⓒ 22

Ⓑ 60   Ⓓ 11

15. Joel has 8 toy cars. Which describes one array he could make using all of his toy cars?

Ⓐ 1 row of 7   Ⓒ 2 rows of 4

Ⓑ 3 rows of 5   Ⓓ 4 rows of 4

16. Calvin drew squares on the sidewalk with chalk. He drew 7 red squares, 7 blue squares, and 7 yellow squares. Which multiplication sentence shows how many squares he drew in all?

Ⓐ $1 \times 7 = 7$

Ⓑ $7 \times 7 = 49$

Ⓒ $1 \times 1 = 1$

Ⓓ $3 \times 7 = 21$

GO ON ➡

17. Each box of crayons has 2 blue crayons and 3 red crayons in it. Danielle has 0 boxes of crayons. Which number sentence shows how many crayons Danielle has?

Ⓐ $0 \times 5 = 0$

Ⓑ $1 \times 5 = 5$

Ⓒ $3 - 2 = 1$

Ⓓ $5 - 5 = 0$

18. Elliot put 4 books on each of 6 bookshelves. Jane put 6 books on each of 4 shelves.

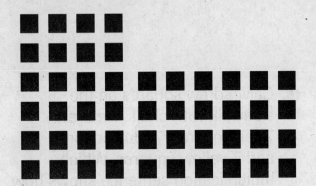

How many books did Elliot and Jane put on the shelves?

Ⓐ 20

Ⓑ 10

Ⓒ 24

Ⓓ 48

19. Alex has 1 basket of eggs. There are 4 brown eggs and 3 white eggs. Which number sentence shows how many eggs Alex has?

Ⓐ $0 \times 7 = 0$

Ⓑ $7 - 1 = 6$

Ⓒ $1 \times 7 = 7$

Ⓓ $7 + 1 = 8$

20. What multiplication sentence does this array show?

Ⓐ $4 \times 3 = 12$

Ⓑ $4 \times 4 = 16$

Ⓒ $4 \times 5 = 20$

Ⓓ $4 \times 6 = 24$

Fill in the bubble for the correct answer.

1. Amelia needs 48 pieces of paper for her art class. She has 5 stacks of paper. Each stack has 9 pieces.

How many more pieces of paper does Amelia need?

Ⓐ 3   Ⓑ 8   Ⓒ 34   Ⓓ 48

2. Ryan has 4 bikes. Each bike has 2 wheels. How many wheels are on all of Ryan's bikes?

Ⓐ 2   Ⓑ 6   Ⓒ 8   Ⓓ 9

3. Angela rides her bike a total of 3 miles to and from school each day. How many miles will she ride in 5 days?

Ⓐ 1   Ⓒ 15
Ⓑ 8   Ⓓ 20

4. Trevor listens to audiobook stories that are each 10 minutes long.

0 5 10 15 20 25 30 35 40 45 50 55 60 65 70

How many minutes does he listen if he listens to 6 stories?

Ⓐ 160
Ⓑ 60
Ⓒ 6
Ⓓ 16

5. Julian makes an array with pennies on a table. He makes 8 rows with 6 pennies in each row. Which shows one way to find the total number of pennies in his array?

Ⓐ (3 + 3) × 6
Ⓑ (8 + 8) × 6
Ⓒ (3 + 4) × 6
Ⓓ (4 + 4) × 6

GO ON

6. A tennis coach carries 5 baskets of tennis balls. Each basket has 8 tennis balls in it. How many tennis balls does the coach carry?

(A) 3   (C) 13

(B) 40   (D) 20

7. There are 4 rows of cars in a parking lot. There are 9 cars in each row. The array shows the parking lot.

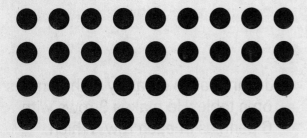

How many cars are in the parking lot?

Record your answer and fill in the bubbles on the grid. Be sure to use the correct place value.

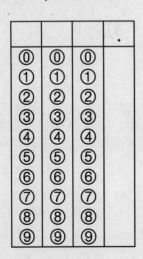

8. Erik has 4 bowls of strawberries. Each bowl has 5 strawberries in it. He gives 5 of the strawberries to his sister. How many strawberries does he have left?

(A) 14   (C) 15

(B) 20   (D) 0

9. Kayla stacked boxes of color pencils in her classroom. She made 5 stacks. Each stack has 6 boxes in it. How many boxes did Kayla stack?

(A) 30   (C) 15

(B) 25   (D) 11

10. Mr. Peters packed 6 boxes of plates. He packed 7 plates in each box. When he got to his new house, he unpacked 3 boxes of plates. How many plates does he have left to unpack?

(A) 16   (C) 42

(B) 24   (D) 21

GO ON

11. Valeria plants 6 rows of trees. She plants 4 trees in each row.

How many trees does she plant?

Ⓐ 24

Ⓑ 28

Ⓒ 10

Ⓓ 12

12. Mr. Murphy has 9 tables in his classroom. One boy and one girl sit at each table. How many boys and girls are in his class?

Ⓐ 9

Ⓑ 18

Ⓒ 21

Ⓓ 11

13. How can you use 2×7 to find 4×7?

Ⓐ $2 \times 7 = 14$ and $14 = 2 \times 7$

Ⓑ $2 \times 7 = 14$ and $7 \times 2 = 14$

Ⓒ $2 \times 7 = 14$ and $14 + 14 = 28$

Ⓓ $2 \times 7 = 14$ and $2 \times 2 = 4$

14. Jordan makes 4 bracelets. She uses 10 inches of string for each bracelet.

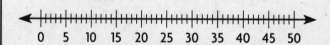

0   5   10   15   20   25   30   35   40   45   50

How many inches of string does she use?

Ⓐ 50   Ⓒ 20

Ⓑ 40   Ⓓ 10

15. Mason buys 4 sandwiches for $3 each. He paid with $20. How much change should Mason receive?

Ⓐ $17   Ⓒ $7

Ⓑ $16   Ⓓ $8

GO ON ➡

16. If Maddie walks 4 miles per hour, how many miles will she walk in 3 hours?

Ⓐ 15 miles

Ⓑ 12 miles

Ⓒ 9 miles

Ⓓ 7 miles

17. Victor paints 6 rows of red squares on his wall. Each row has 5 squares. Then he decides to change 8 of the squares to blue.

How many squares will still be red?

Ⓐ 22

Ⓑ 40

Ⓒ 30

Ⓓ 24

18. Ana bakes 6 trays of muffins. Each tray holds 8 muffins.

How many muffins does she bake?

Ⓐ 42   Ⓒ 48

Ⓑ 14   Ⓓ 24

19. Mrs. Chang made booties for 8 dogs in her neighborhood. Each dog has 4 booties. How many booties do the dogs have in all?

Ⓐ 32 Ⓑ 24 Ⓒ 40 Ⓓ 28

20. Antonio has 3 ribbons that are each 8 inches long. He has another ribbon that is 9 inches long. How many inches of ribbon does he have?

Ⓐ 20 Ⓑ 75 Ⓒ 27 Ⓓ 33

STOP

Name _____

Fill in the bubble for the correct answer.

1. An octopus has 8 tentacles.

0 2 4 6 8 10 12 14 16 18 20 22 24 26 28 30

How many tentacles do
3 octopuses have?

Ⓐ 30   Ⓒ 16

Ⓑ 24   Ⓓ 20

2. There are 3 baskets of apples on
each of 3 shelves. Each basket has
8 apples. How many apples are on
the shelves?

Ⓐ 14   Ⓒ 72

Ⓑ 9   Ⓓ 24

3. Alejandro has 7 bags of marbles.
Each bag has 3 red marbles and 2
blue marbles. How many marbles
does Alejandro have in all?

Ⓐ 35   Ⓒ 12

Ⓑ 21   Ⓓ 42

4. A tricycle has 3 wheels. How many
wheels do 9 tricycles have?

Ⓐ 9

Ⓑ 30

Ⓒ 24

Ⓓ 27

5. Caleb made a number pattern.

4, 8, 12, 16, 20, 24

Which describes Caleb's pattern?

Ⓐ Multiply by 4.

Ⓑ Multiply by 2.

Ⓒ Add 4.

Ⓓ Add 2.

GO ON ➡

6. Danielle made 8 bracelets. Each bracelet has 7 beads. How many beads did Danielle use?

Ⓐ 56　　Ⓒ 42

Ⓑ 48　　Ⓓ 15

7. Adrian has 7 model airplanes. Each model airplane has 4 wings. How many wings are on Adrian's models?

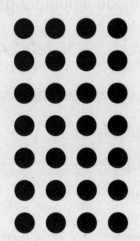

Ⓐ 21　　Ⓒ 24

Ⓑ 11　　Ⓓ 28

8. Evelyn spends $9 each week for school lunch. How much does she spend in 5 weeks?

Ⓐ $36　　Ⓒ $45

Ⓑ $40　　Ⓓ $54

9. Luis has saved $4 every week for 7 weeks. How many more weeks will he have to save to have $36?

Ⓐ 1

Ⓑ 2

Ⓒ 6

Ⓓ 8

10. Joseph has 6 boxes. Each box has 9 books in it. How many books does he have in all the boxes?

Record your answer and fill in the bubbles on the grid. Be sure to use the correct place value.

⓪	⓪	⓪	.
①	①	①	
②	②	②	
③	③	③	
④	④	④	
⑤	⑤	⑤	
⑥	⑥	⑥	
⑦	⑦	⑦	
⑧	⑧	⑧	
⑨	⑨	⑨	

GO ON

11. Briana has 3 hours of soccer practice 2 days a week.

How many hours of practice will Briana have in 2 weeks?

Ⓐ 5   Ⓒ 6

Ⓑ 10   Ⓓ 12

12. Christopher has 6 boxes of pencils. Each box has 8 pencils. How many pencils does he have?

Ⓐ 48   Ⓒ 63

Ⓑ 56   Ⓓ 72

13. Stella is making banners for her school. For each banner, she needs 3 yards of red fabric and 4 yards of blue fabric. What is the total number of yards of fabric she needs to make 5 banners?

Ⓐ 17   Ⓒ 35

Ⓑ 60   Ⓓ 12

14. Rita makes 7 party invitations. She uses 3 sheets of paper for each invitation.

How many sheets of paper does she use for the invitations?

Ⓐ 14   Ⓒ 24

Ⓑ 21   Ⓓ 18

15. Which of the following describes this pattern?

6, 12, 18, 24, 30, 36

Ⓐ Add 12.

Ⓑ Add 6.

Ⓒ Multiply by 6.

Ⓓ Multiply by 12.

GO ON

16. Matt drew 8 pictures. He drew 4 stars in each picture.

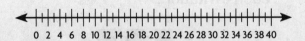

0 2 4 6 8 10 12 14 16 18 20 22 24 26 28 30 32 34 36 38 40

How many stars did Matt draw?

(A) 36   (C) 40

(B) 24   (D) 32

17. Ava makes 7 necklaces. She uses 3 round beads, 2 square beads, and 4 oval beads for each necklace. How many beads does she use?

(A) 63   (C) 24

(B) 27   (D) 35

18. A penguin has 2 wings. How many wings do 9 penguins have?

(A) 11   (C) 18

(B) 27   (D) 16

19. Julian babysits his cousins 3 times a week. Each time he babysits for 3 hours and earns $5 per hour. How much does Julian earn each week?

(A) $11

(B) $45

(C) $30

(D) $24

20. Molly puts 5 photos on each page in her scrapbook. She makes the table to find out how many photos she needs to fill 6 pages. Which pattern do the products show?

x	1	2	3	4	5	6
5	5	10	15	20	25	30

(A) even, then odd, then repeat

(B) odd, then even, then repeat

(C) all odd

(D) all even

Name _____

Fill in the bubble for the correct answer.

1. There are 15 shelves of juice at a grocery store. Each shelf has 8 bottles of juice.

How many bottles of juice are on the shelves?

Ⓐ 48

Ⓑ 100

Ⓒ 80

Ⓓ 120

2. Students at Leland Elementary School are separated into 2 groups to go on a field trip. Each group needs 3 buses. There are 30 students on each bus. The Commutative Property can help you multiply. Which shows the Commutative Property?

Ⓐ 2 × 3 × 30 = (2 × 3) × 30

Ⓑ 2 × 3 × 30 = 3 × 2 × 30

Ⓒ 2 × 3 × 30 = (2 × 3 × 30)

Ⓓ 2 × 3 × 30 = (2 × 30) × 3

3. Emily will ride her bike 20 minutes each day for 7 days. How many minutes will she ride in all?

Ⓐ 140 minutes

Ⓑ 100 minutes

Ⓒ 27 minutes

Ⓓ 70 minutes

4. Julia makes 6 wreaths from peanut shells. She uses 52 peanut shells for each wreath. How many peanut shells will she use?

Ⓐ 302

Ⓑ 322

Ⓒ 312

Ⓓ 300

5. Casey spends $30 each month on school lunch. How much will she spend on lunches for 7 months?

Ⓐ $21

Ⓑ $210

Ⓒ $150

Ⓓ $100

GO ON →

6. There are 2 vases of flowers on each of 2 tables in a restaurant. Each vase has 40 flowers. The Associative Property can help you multiply. Which shows the Associative Property?

Ⓐ $(2 \times 2) \times 40 = 2 \times (2 \times 40)$

Ⓑ $2 \times 2 \times 40 = 2 \times 2 \times 40$

Ⓒ $2 \times 2 \times 40 = 40 \times 2 \times 2$

Ⓓ $2 \times 2 \times 40 = (2 \times 20) + (2 \times 20)$

7. There are 5 rows of cars parked in a parking lot. There are 30 cars in each row. How many cars are parked in the parking lot?

Ⓐ 25

Ⓑ 100

Ⓒ 140

Ⓓ 150

8. Christina buys 4 shirts for $17 each. What is the total cost of the shirts?

Record your answer and fill in the bubbles on the grid. Be sure to use the correct place value.

⓪	⓪	⓪	.
①	①	①	
②	②	②	
③	③	③	
④	④	④	
⑤	⑤	⑤	
⑥	⑥	⑥	
⑦	⑦	⑦	
⑧	⑧	⑧	
⑨	⑨	⑨	

9. There are 8 swim meets. At each meet, 16 volunteers are needed to keep time. How many time keepers are needed for all of the meets?

Ⓐ 24   Ⓒ 128

Ⓑ 48   Ⓓ 80

10. Talia buys 3 books for $20 each and 3 books for $30 each. How much does she spend on the books?

Ⓐ $30   Ⓒ $90

Ⓑ $150   Ⓓ $60

GO ON

11. Duncan puts muffins on 7 plates for a carnival. Each plate has 20 muffins. How many muffins does he put on the plates?

Ⓐ 120

Ⓑ 130

Ⓒ 150

Ⓓ 140

12. There are 8 boxes of apples in the barn at an apple orchard. There are 30 apples in each box.

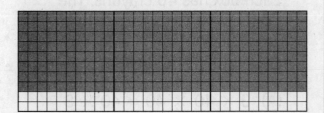

How many apples are in the boxes?

Ⓐ 240

Ⓑ 300

Ⓒ 160

Ⓓ 250

13. There are 4 shelves with 35 books on each shelf in one section of a library. There are 3 shelves with 25 books on each shelf in a different section.

How many books are in these two sections of the library?

Ⓐ 240

Ⓑ 215

Ⓒ 60

Ⓓ 140

14. Nicholas buys 4 packs of chewing gum. Each pack has 20 pieces. How many pieces of gum does he buy?

Ⓐ 24   Ⓒ 60

Ⓑ 100   Ⓓ 80

15. A large bag of rice costs $5. How much will 40 bags of rice cost?

Ⓐ $200   Ⓒ $160

Ⓑ $180   Ⓓ $240

GO ON ➡

16. There are 4 third grade classes at West Elementary School. Each class has 26 students.

How many students are in third grade at West Elementary School?

(A) 84   (C) 30

(B) 104   (D) 120

17. All the athletes lined up in 5 rows of 60 at the beginning of a triathlon. How many athletes were there in all?

(A) 400   (C) 250

(B) 150   (D) 300

18. There are 32 runners from each of 8 schools at a track meet. How many runners are at the track meet?

(A) 56   (C) 256

(B) 255   (D) 246

19. Ms. Tervo buys 6 packages of hot dog buns for a school picnic. Each package has 16 buns. At the end of the picnic, there are 12 buns leftover. How many buns were used at the picnic?

(A) 84

(B) 96

(C) 48

(D) 24

20. Caroline has 3 boxes of crayons. Each box has 40 crayons. The Distributive Property can help you multiply. Which shows the Distributive Property?

(A) $3 \times 40 \times 40 = 40 \times 3$

(B) $3 \times 40 = (3 \times 20) + (3 \times 20)$

(C) $3 \times 40 = 40 + 40 + 40$

(D) $3 \times 40 = (3 \times 40)$

STOP

Fill in the bubble for the correct answer.

1. An art teacher hands out 42 charcoal pencils. Each student gets 6 pencils.

How many students are in the art class?

Ⓐ 6   Ⓒ 9

Ⓑ 7   Ⓓ 8

2. Elena has 24 marbles. She wants to put them in groups of 8. How many groups will she make?

Ⓐ 5   Ⓒ 3

Ⓑ 4   Ⓓ 6

3. Josh has 45 toy cars. He takes out 13 of them. He lines up the rest in 4 equal rows. How many cars are in each row?

Ⓐ 8   Ⓒ 7

Ⓑ 5   Ⓓ 6

4. Katie planted 45 cucumber plants with 9 plants in each row.

How many rows of cucumber plants did she plant?

Ⓐ 54

Ⓑ 6

Ⓒ 4

Ⓓ 5

5. There are 12 board games in 3 equal stacks. How many board games are in each stack?

Ⓐ 2

Ⓑ 4

Ⓒ 3

Ⓓ 5

GO ON

6. Alexa brings a bag of 24 apples to a picnic. Dylan brings a bag of 18 apples. They divide all of the apples equally into 6 bowls. How many apples are in each bowl?

Ⓐ 7

Ⓑ 1

Ⓒ 3

Ⓓ 8

7. Isaac melts 30 crayons to make candles. He uses 6 crayons to make each candle.

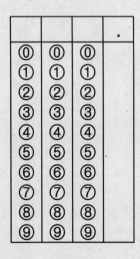

How many candles does he make?

Record your answer and fill in the bubbles on the grid. Be sure to use the correct place value.

8. Adam's family packs snacks for a hike. They divide 8 apples and 12 bananas equally among 4 people.

How many pieces of fruit does each person get?

Ⓐ 3   Ⓑ 20   Ⓒ 2   Ⓓ 5

9. Mariana puts 18 stuffed animals on her shelves. There are 6 stuffed animals on each shelf. How many shelves does she use?

Ⓐ 3   Ⓑ 9   Ⓒ 24   Ⓓ 2

10. At a taco shop, 20 tacos were sold during lunch and 16 tacos were sold during dinner. Each customer ordered 4 tacos.

How many customers bought tacos?

Ⓐ 8   Ⓑ 9   Ⓒ 4   Ⓓ 5

GO ON

11. Eduardo has 24 glass beads. He wants to put the same number of beads on each of the 4 bracelets he is making.

How many beads will be on each bracelet?

(A) 20   (C) 6

(B) 3   (D) 8

12. Nathaniel packs 28 new shirts into boxes to ship to a store. He packs 7 shirts in each box. How many boxes does he use?

(A) 3   (C) 4

(B) 5   (D) 9

13. Jonathan has 54 apple slices. He divides them equally into 6 bowls. How many apple slices are in each bowl?

(A) 8   (C) 7

(B) 5   (D) 9

14. Ms. Cartwright is hanging 24 pieces of student artwork in the hallway. She plans to hang the art in 3 rows with the same number of pieces in each row. She has already hung 2 rows.

How many pieces of art does she have left to hang?

(A) 8

(B) 4

(C) 5

(D) 12

15. Morgan makes 25 pancakes. She puts the same number of pancakes on each of 5 plates. How many pancakes does Morgan put on each plate?

(A) 4

(B) 5

(C) 20

(D) 6

GO ON

16. Audrey puts 32 strawberries in 4 bowls for a party. She puts the same number of strawberries in each bowl.

How many strawberries are in each bowl?

Ⓐ 9

Ⓑ 7

Ⓒ 8

Ⓓ 10

17. Allison collects 24 red leaves and 24 yellow leaves. She presses them between wax paper, making 6 sheets of leaves with the same number on each sheet. How many leaves does she press on each sheet?

Ⓐ 3

Ⓑ 7

Ⓒ 4

Ⓓ 8

18. Landon has 36 pecans for himself and his friends. He eats 4 of them. Then he gives 4 pecans each to some of his friends until they are all gone. To how many friends does Landon give pecans?

Ⓐ 9   Ⓒ 10

Ⓑ 8   Ⓓ 7

19. Diana makes an array using 72 postage stamps. If she puts 9 stamps in each row, how many rows does she make?

Ⓐ 8

Ⓑ 6

Ⓒ 9

Ⓓ 7

20. Michael uses 12 cups of pumpkin to make pumpkin muffins. Each batch of muffins needs 2 cups of pumpkin. How many batches of muffins does Michael make?

Ⓐ 5

Ⓑ 4

Ⓒ 10

Ⓓ 6

Fill in the bubble for the correct answer.

1. Elizabeth has some oranges. She gives 1 orange to each of her friends. She gives away 7 oranges. To how many friends does she give oranges?

   Ⓐ 6   Ⓒ 8

   Ⓑ 5   Ⓓ 7

2. Which set of numbers contains all even numbers?

   Ⓐ 48, 64, 92

   Ⓑ 21, 35, 41

   Ⓒ 38, 46, 51

   Ⓓ 22, 67, 84

3. Mae bought 42 paintbrushes. The paintbrushes came in packages of 6. Which equation gives the related fact for the number of packages of paintbrushes Mae bought?

   Ⓐ $42 \div 2 = 21$

   Ⓑ $6 \times 7 = 42$

   Ⓒ $14 \times 3 = 14$

   Ⓓ $42 \div 3 = 14$

4. Elena has 27 classmates. Which statement is true about the number 27?

   Ⓐ It is even because there is a 2 in the tens place.

   Ⓑ It is even because there is a 7 in the ones place.

   Ⓒ It is odd because there is a 2 in the tens place.

   Ⓓ It is odd because there is a 7 in the ones place.

5. Molly has 8 necklaces. She hangs each necklace on its own hook. How many hooks does Molly use?

   Ⓐ 9

   Ⓑ 10

   Ⓒ 8

   Ⓓ 7

GO ON

6. Eli has 36 books. He places the same number of books on each of 9 shelves. Which related fact could be used to find the number of books on each shelf?

Ⓐ 4 × 9 = 36

Ⓑ 36 ÷ 6 = 6

Ⓒ 6 × 6 = 36

Ⓓ 36 × 9 = 324

7. Will has 8 plates and 0 cookies.

How many cookies can he put on each plate?

Ⓐ 1   Ⓒ 8

Ⓑ 7   Ⓓ 0

8. Use the clues to find the number of marbles Al has. The number is odd and has 2 digits. The sum of the digits is 6. The digit in the tens place is greater than 0 and less than 4. How many marbles does Al have?

Ⓐ 32   Ⓒ 24

Ⓑ 33   Ⓓ 35

9. Claire has 6 hermit crabs. She puts each hermit crab in its own bowl. How many bowls does Claire use?

Ⓐ 7

Ⓑ 1

Ⓒ 6

Ⓓ 5

10. Jason has 58 baseball cards. Which statement is true about the number 58?

Ⓐ It is odd because there is a 5 in the tens place.

Ⓑ It is odd because there is a 8 in the ones place.

Ⓒ It is even because there is a 5 in the tens place.

Ⓓ It is even because there is a 8 in the ones place.

GO ON

11. Which equation is **NOT** included in the same set of related facts as $3 \times 8 = 24$?

Ⓐ $6 \times 4 = 24$

Ⓑ $24 \div 3 = 8$

Ⓒ $24 \div 8 = 3$

Ⓓ $8 \times 3 = 24$

12. There are 12 people who want to buy tickets to a concert. There are 0 tickets available. Which equation describes how many tickets each person can buy?

Ⓐ $12 \div 1 = 12$

Ⓑ $12 + 0 = 12$

Ⓒ $0 \div 12 = 0$

Ⓓ $0 \times 12 = 0$

13. Use the clues to find the number of pencils Caleb has. The number is even and has 2 digits. The sum of the digits is 10. The digit in the ones place is greater than 0 and less than 5. How many pencils does Caleb have?

Ⓐ 28   Ⓒ 37

Ⓑ 82   Ⓓ 53

14. Sydney has some dogs. She gives each dog 1 treat. If she gives the dogs 6 treats, how many dogs does she have?

Record your answer and fill in the bubbles on the grid. Be sure to use the correct place value.

⓪	⓪	⓪	·
①	①	①	
②	②	②	
③	③	③	
④	④	④	
⑤	⑤	⑤	
⑥	⑥	⑥	
⑦	⑦	⑦	
⑧	⑧	⑧	
⑨	⑨	⑨	

15. There are 24 students sitting at 6 tables. Which equation gives the related fact for the number of students at each table?

Ⓐ $24 \div 8 = 3$

Ⓑ $4 \times 6 = 24$

Ⓒ $24 \div 3 = 8$

Ⓓ $8 \times 3 = 24$

GO ON

16. James gives 6 grapes to each of 9 friends. Which equation gives a related fact for the number of grapes James gives to his friends?

Ⓐ 54 ÷ 9 = 6

Ⓑ 18 × 3 = 54

Ⓒ 54 ÷ 3 = 18

Ⓓ 3 × 18 = 54

17. Which set of numbers contains all odd numbers?

Ⓐ 121, 327, 614

Ⓑ 518, 457, 606

Ⓒ 231, 355, 817

Ⓓ 202, 187, 443

18. Nicole has some rose bushes. Each bush has 1 rose. There are 9 roses.

How many rose bushes does Nicole have?

Ⓐ 9   Ⓒ 8

Ⓑ 7   Ⓓ 0

19. There are 16 students in Ms. Hernandez's class. Which is true about the number 16?

Ⓐ It is odd because there is a 1 in the tens place.

Ⓑ It is odd because there is a 6 in the ones place.

Ⓒ It is even because there is a 1 in the tens place.

Ⓓ It is even because there is a 6 in the ones place.

20. Molly wrote an equation to show how many beads she needed to make nine bracelets. Which equation is **NOT** included in the same set of related facts as 8 × 9 = 72?

Ⓐ 9 × 8 = 72

Ⓑ 4 × 18 = 72

Ⓒ 72 ÷ 9 = 8

Ⓓ 72 ÷ 8 = 9

STOP

Fill in the bubble for the correct answer.

1. Michael brought 20 muffins to a bake sale. Eva brought 20 muffins. Together they sold 10 muffins every hour until there were none left. For how many hours did they sell muffins?

Ⓐ 1 hour   Ⓒ 4 hours

Ⓑ 2 hours   Ⓓ 3 hours

2. José gives each person at a party 2 clues to a treasure hunt. He has 12 clues. How many people are at the party?

Ⓐ 8   Ⓒ 14

Ⓑ 6   Ⓓ 10

3. Abby has 16 tomato slices. She puts the same number of tomato slices on each of 4 sandwiches. How many tomato slices does Abby put on each sandwich?

Ⓐ 4   Ⓒ 2

Ⓑ 5   Ⓓ 3

4. Anthony has a photo book with 40 photos. It has 5 photos on each page.

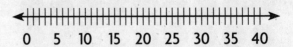

How many pages in the book have photos?

Ⓐ 35

Ⓑ 6

Ⓒ 9

Ⓓ 8

5. Victoria bakes 9 biscuits to put on 3 lunch plates she will deliver. She puts the same number of biscuits on each plate. How many biscuits are on each plate?

Ⓐ 3

Ⓑ 4

Ⓒ 2

Ⓓ 6

GO ON

6. There are 12 red shirts and 33 yellow shirts at a store. A salesperson puts 5 shirts in each stack on a shelf.

How many stacks of t-shirts are on the shelf?

Ⓐ 2

Ⓑ 7

Ⓒ 9

Ⓓ 8

7. Olivia has 18 stuffed animals in 2 baskets in her room.

Each basket has the same number of stuffed animals. How many stuffed animals are in each basket?

Ⓐ 6

Ⓑ 9

Ⓒ 8

Ⓓ 16

8. Andy sold 60 watermelons at the farmers' market on Saturday. He sold 10 watermelons every hour. For how many hours did Andy sell watermelons?

Ⓐ 6   Ⓒ 12

Ⓑ 4   Ⓓ 50

9. Carlos has 28 color photos in 4 equal rows in his scrapbook. He has 20 black and white photos in 4 equal rows.

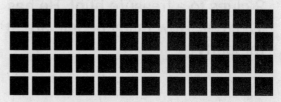

How many more color photos than black and white photos are in each row?

Ⓐ 3   Ⓒ 7

Ⓑ 2   Ⓓ 5

10. Leslie puts 21 chocolate granola bars and 6 peanut butter granola bars into plastic bags for snacks. She puts 3 granola bars into each plastic bag. How many plastic bags does she use?

Ⓐ 8   Ⓒ 9

Ⓑ 7   Ⓓ 2

GO ON

11. Emily folds her socks in groups of 2 to make pairs. She folds 16 socks. How many pairs of socks does she fold?

(A) 7   (C) 14

(B) 6   (D) 8

12. Ethan has 32 loaves of bread. He puts the same number of loaves of bread in each of 4 baskets.

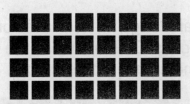

How many loaves of bread does he put in each basket?

Record your answer and fill in the bubbles on the grid. Be sure to use the correct place value.

⓪	⓪	⓪	•
①	①	①	
②	②	②	
③	③	③	
④	④	④	
⑤	⑤	⑤	
⑥	⑥	⑥	
⑦	⑦	⑦	
⑧	⑧	⑧	
⑨	⑨	⑨	

13. Jade pays $27 for 3 books. Each book costs the same amount. She pays $21 for 3 journals. Each journal costs the same amount.

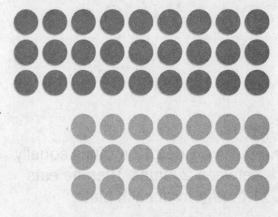

How much more does she pay for a book than for a journal?

(A) $2   (B) $6   (C) $7   (D) $9

14. Jasmine pays $40 for 5 shirts. Each shirt costs the same amount. How much does each shirt cost?

(A) $35   (B) $8   (C) $5   (D) $7

15. There are 40 students in gym class. They are divided into teams of 10 students. How many teams are there?

(A) 4   (B) 6   (C) 30   (D) 5

GO ON

16. Lexi makes 14 blankets. She makes the same number of blue blankets as red blankets. How many blankets are blue?

Ⓐ 4   Ⓒ 8

Ⓑ 7   Ⓓ 6

17. Aaron divides 12 muffins equally between 2 plates. Then he eats 1 muffin from each plate.

How many muffins are left on each plate?

Ⓐ 5   Ⓒ 4

Ⓑ 6   Ⓓ 3

18. Andrea listens to music for 70 minutes. Every 10 minutes, she changes the type of music. How many different types of music does she listen to?

Ⓐ 10   Ⓒ 8

Ⓑ 6   Ⓓ 7

19. Meg has 40 pears and 20 peaches. She divides them equally among 10 baskets. How many pieces of fruit does she put in each basket?

Ⓐ 4

Ⓑ 2

Ⓒ 6

Ⓓ 10

20. Noah hangs 21 necklaces on 3 hooks. Each hook has the same number of necklaces.

How many necklaces does he hang on each hook?

Ⓐ 5

Ⓑ 7

Ⓒ 21

Ⓓ 18

STOP

Name _____

Fill in the bubble for the correct answer.

1. Michelle has 30 stickers. She divides the stickers equally onto 6 sheets of paper. How many stickers are on each sheet of paper?

   (A) 4   (C) 5

   (B) 6   (D) 3

2. There are 36 children on the playground. The same number of children are playing at each of the 9 slides. How many children are at each slide?

   (A) 4   (C) 27

   (B) 41   (D) 5

3. Aaron sees 4 stop signs. He counts 32 sides in all.

   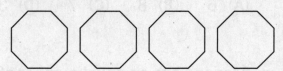

   How many sides are on one sign?

   (A) 6   (C) 4

   (B) 8   (D) 7

4. Trina swam 28 days in a row. There are 7 days in a week. For how many weeks did she swim every day?

   (A) 4

   (B) 21

   (C) 3

   (D) 5

5. Mae divides 24 carrots equally among 8 rabbits.

   How many carrots will each rabbit get?

   (A) 4

   (B) 18

   (C) 2

   (D) 3

GO ON

6. Cameron's friends and family are traveling. Each car can seat 6 people. There are 24 people.

How many cars will they need?

Ⓐ 18

Ⓑ 3

Ⓒ 4

Ⓓ 8

7. There are 15 girls and 15 boys in Ms. Haverly's class. If an equal number of students sit at each of 5 tables, how many tables are in Ms. Haverly's classroom?

Ⓐ 5

Ⓑ 6

Ⓒ 7

Ⓓ 3

8. Ella picked 9 cucumbers from each of her cucumber plants. She picked 54 cucumbers in all. She picked 9 tomatoes from each of her tomato plants. She picked 36 tomatoes in all. How many more cucumber plants than tomato plants does she have?

Ⓐ 4   Ⓑ 2   Ⓒ 6   Ⓓ 10

9. There are 42 children playing soccer at a park. Each team has 7 players.

How many teams are there?

Ⓐ 6   Ⓑ 8   Ⓒ 7   Ⓓ 35

10. Mariana has an equal number of yellow, green, blue, red, white, and black building blocks. She has 48 blocks. How many of each color block does she have?

Ⓐ 12   Ⓒ 6

Ⓑ 8   Ⓓ 4

GO ON ➡

11. Xavier bought 56 bagels. Bagels come in bags of 8 bagels each.

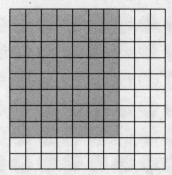

How many bags of bagels did he buy?

Record your answer and fill in the bubbles on the grid. Be sure to use the correct place value.

⓪	⓪	⓪	.
①	①	①	
②	②	②	
③	③	③	
④	④	④	
⑤	⑤	⑤	
⑥	⑥	⑥	
⑦	⑦	⑦	
⑧	⑧	⑧	
⑨	⑨	⑨	

12. There are 21 cars and 14 vans parked in a parking lot. They are parked in rows of 7. How many vehicles are in each row?

Ⓐ 7

Ⓑ 3

Ⓒ 2

Ⓓ 5

13. Mr. Martino separates 63 students into 9 equal teams for a quiz bowl. How many students are on each team?

Ⓐ 54   Ⓒ 9

Ⓑ 7   Ⓓ 8

14. Jesse bought 5 boxes of granola bars. Over the next few days, he ate 4 granola bars. Now he has 21 granola bars. How many granola bars were in each box?

Ⓐ 7   Ⓒ 5

Ⓑ 4   Ⓓ 3

15. Julia bought 36 tennis balls. There are 6 tennis balls in each can.

How many cans did she buy?

Ⓐ 6   Ⓒ 8

Ⓑ 4   Ⓓ 9

GO ON

16. Hector has 32 notecards. They are in packages of 8.

How many packages of notecards does he have?

Ⓐ 8   Ⓒ 4

Ⓑ 5   Ⓓ 3

17. Logan has 63 marbles. He has 9 marbles of each color. How many different colors of marbles does Logan have?

Ⓐ 5   Ⓒ 6

Ⓑ 8   Ⓓ 7

18. Jocelyn has 3 bags of oranges. Each bag has 8 oranges. She divides the oranges evenly into 4 bowls at a picnic. How many oranges does she put in each bowl?

Ⓐ 5   Ⓒ 8

Ⓑ 15   Ⓓ 6

19. Haley divides 72 grapes equally into 9 bowls.

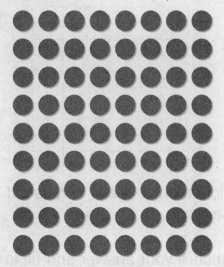

How many grapes are in each bowl?

Ⓐ 8   Ⓒ 4

Ⓑ 5   Ⓓ 3

20. Jordan counts 40 goldfish at the pet store. There are 8 goldfish in each tank.

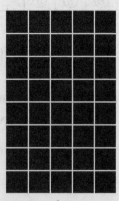

How many tanks are there?

Ⓐ 8   Ⓒ 4

Ⓑ 5   Ⓓ 3

STOP

Name _____

Fill in the bubble for the correct answer.

1. Ellen puts 8 peaches into each of 3 baskets.

If she has 28 peaches, how many peaches are leftover?

Ⓐ 3   Ⓒ 17

Ⓑ 4   Ⓓ 9

2. It takes Theo 9 days to choose pictures for a photo book. If he chooses 9 photos each day, how many photos does he choose in all?

Ⓐ 81   Ⓒ 72

Ⓑ 63   Ⓓ 54

3. Dana has 16 balls in 2 baskets.

There is an equal number of balls in each basket. How many balls are in each basket?

Ⓐ 9   Ⓒ 7

Ⓑ 18   Ⓓ 8

4. Trevor makes an array using 54 stickers. If he puts 6 stickers in each row, how many rows does he make?

Ⓐ 9

Ⓑ 5

Ⓒ 7

Ⓓ 8

5. Alyssa has 3 plants. Each plant has 5 leaves.

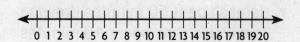

How many leaves do the plants have in all?

Ⓐ 8

Ⓑ 16

Ⓒ 14

Ⓓ Not here

GO ON ➡

6. There are 24 trees along the sidewalk of Brianna's school. Which is true about the number 24?

Ⓐ It is even because there is a 2 in the tens place.

Ⓑ It is even because there is a 4 in the ones place.

Ⓒ It is odd because there is a 2 in the tens place.

Ⓓ It is odd because there is a 4 in the ones place.

7. James spent 50 minutes drawing last week. If he spent 10 minutes drawing each day, how many days did he draw last week?

Ⓐ 5

Ⓑ 6

Ⓒ 60

Ⓓ 40

8. Chloe has 4 bags of marbles. Each bag has 40 marbles. How many marbles does Chloe have?

Ⓐ 120   Ⓒ 160

Ⓑ 150   Ⓓ 44

9. How can you use 2×5 to find 4×5?

Ⓐ $2 \times 5 = 10$ and $10 = 2 \times 5$

Ⓑ $2 \times 5 = 10$ and $10 + 10 = 20$

Ⓒ $2 \times 5 = 10$ and $5 \times 2 = 10$

Ⓓ $2 \times 5 = 10$ and $2 \times 2 = 4$

10. Isaiah has walked 3 miles every day for 8 days. How many more days will he have to walk to reach a total of 33 miles?

Ⓐ 5   Ⓒ 4

Ⓑ 3   Ⓓ 11

GO ON

11. Caleb has 20 seeds to plant. He plants the same number of seeds in 4 rows.

How many seeds does he plant in each row?

(A) 9   (C) 4

(B) 3   (D) 5

12. Ms. Callen's students stack their math books on 3 shelves. They put 9 books on each shelf. How many books are on the shelves?

(A) 27   (C) 21

(B) 18   (D) 12

13. Eduardo rides his bike 18 miles each day for 6 days on a trip.

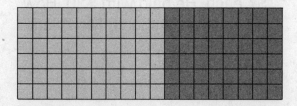

How many miles does he ride his bike in all?

(A) 348   (C) 108

(B) 68   (D) 648

14. Amanda makes 6 stuffed bears. She sews 2 eyes on each bear. How many eyes does Amanda sew on in all?

(A) 16

(B) 12

(C) 8

(D) 10

15. Which set of numbers contains all odd numbers?

(A) 366, 208, 416

(B) 205, 317, 143

(C) 358, 127, 581

(D) 499, 519, 820

GO ON

16. Nevaeh has 15 cups of blueberries. He freezes 6 cups of blueberries. Then he uses the rest to make pies.

If he uses 3 cups of blueberries in each pie, how many pies does he make?

Ⓐ 3   Ⓑ 24   Ⓒ 27   Ⓓ 9

17. Meg mixes 6 teaspoons of cinnamon and 21 teaspoons of sugar together. She puts 3 teaspoons of the mixture into each of a number of containers. How many containers does she use?

Ⓐ 2   Ⓑ 9   Ⓒ 7   Ⓓ 4

18. There are 27 cars on an amusement park ride. If 4 people can fit in each car, how many people can go on the ride?

Ⓐ 98   Ⓒ 99

Ⓑ 88   Ⓓ 108

19. Hayden has green and blue cubes. Five cubes are green and the rest are blue. He makes 4 cube trains with six cubes in each train.

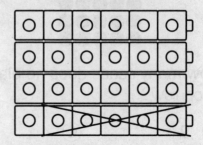

How many blue cubes are there?

Record your answer and fill in the bubbles on the grid. Be sure to use the correct place value.

⓪	⓪	⓪	.
①	①	①	
②	②	②	
③	③	③	
④	④	④	
⑤	⑤	⑤	
⑥	⑥	⑥	
⑦	⑦	⑦	
⑧	⑧	⑧	
⑨	⑨	⑨	

20. Mr. Allen bought 3 fish for $7 each. He paid with $30. How much change should Mr. Allen receive?

Ⓐ $11   Ⓒ $9

Ⓑ $19   Ⓓ $37

GO ON

21. Natalia made 7 paper flowers. Each flower has 8 petals.

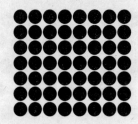

How many petals do the flowers have in all?

Ⓐ 48   Ⓑ 56   Ⓒ 54   Ⓓ 15

22. Riley has 3 drawers with 6 shirts in each drawer. Which equation gives a related fact for the number of shirts Riley has?

Ⓐ $18 \div 6 = 3$ Ⓒ $18 \div 2 = 9$

Ⓑ $9 \times 2 = 18$ Ⓓ $2 \times 9 = 18$

23. Cesar is sorting 48 books. He sorts an equal number of books into each of 6 bins. He has already filled 3 bins.

How many books does he have left to sort?

Ⓐ 18   Ⓑ 2   Ⓒ 8   Ⓓ 24

24. There are 5 shelves of shoes in the back room of a shoe store. There are 40 boxes on each shelf. There are 2 shoes in each box. The Associative Property of Multiplication can help you solve for the total number of shoes. Which shows the Associative Property?

Ⓐ $2 \times (5 \times 40) = (2 \times 5) \times 40$

Ⓑ $2 \times 5 \times 40 = 2 \times 40 \times 5$

Ⓒ $2 \times 5 \times 40 = 2 \times 5 \times 40$

Ⓓ $2 \times 5 \times 40 = 5 \times 2 \times 40$

25. Mario has 8 boxes of pencils. There are 8 pencils in each box. How many pencils does Mario have?

Ⓐ 56

Ⓑ 63

Ⓒ 64

Ⓓ 72

GO ON

26. Which multiplication sentence does this array show?

(A) $5 \times 8 = 40$

(B) $5 \times 5 = 25$

(C) $5 \times 6 = 30$

(D) $5 \times 7 = 35$

27. Mr. Jones is packing pears in boxes to ship to stores. He packs 30 pears in each box. How many pears will he pack in 8 boxes?

(A) 80   (C) 38

(B) 240   (D) 160

28. There are 30 girls that play soccer and 40 boys that play soccer. Each team has 10 players. How many soccer teams are there?

(A) 7   (C) 4

(B) 3   (D) 8

29. Giselle divides 54 sheets of paper equally into 6 stacks.

How many sheets of paper does she put in each stack?

Record your answer and fill in the bubbles on the grid. Be sure to use the correct place value.

⓪	⓪	⓪	.
①	①	①	
②	②	②	
③	③	③	
④	④	④	
⑤	⑤	⑤	
⑥	⑥	⑥	
⑦	⑦	⑦	
⑧	⑧	⑧	
⑨	⑨	⑨	

30. Daisy has 16 crayons. Which describes one array she could make using all of her crayons?

(A) 5 rows of 3   (C) 3 rows of 4

(B) 2 rows of 7   (D) 2 rows of 8

STOP

Fill in the bubble for the correct answer.

1. Jen has 72 apples to put in gift baskets. She puts the same number of apples in each basket.

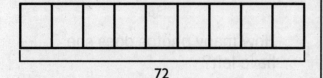

72

If there are 9 baskets, how many apples does Jen put in each basket?

Ⓐ 7

Ⓑ 9

Ⓒ 8

Ⓓ 6

2. There are 174 students in first grade, 108 students in second grade, and 163 students in third grade at Tom's school. How many more second and third graders are there than first graders?

Ⓐ 97

Ⓑ 271

Ⓒ 107

Ⓓ 103

3. Leni baked 12 blueberry muffins in a muffin pan. The pan has 3 rows. If each row of the pan has the same number of muffins, how many muffins are in each row?

Ⓐ 2   Ⓒ 4

Ⓑ 3   Ⓓ 6

4. Victor needs 7 pieces of wood for each birdhouse.

Birdhouses	1	2	3	4	5
Pieces of Wood	7	14	21	28	

How many pieces of wood does he need to make 5 birdhouses?

Ⓐ 42   Ⓒ 7

Ⓑ 35   Ⓓ 33

5. June saves $4. Maddie saves 3 times as much. Which expression represents the amount of money Maddie saves compared to June?

Ⓐ 4 + 3   Ⓒ 3 + 3 + 3

Ⓑ 3 × 3   Ⓓ 3 × 4

GO ON

6. It is 97 miles from Alana's house to her aunt's house. Alana's family left their house and drove 34 miles. They took a break and then they drove 38 more miles.

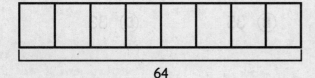

How many miles do they have left to drive?

- (A) 63
- (B) 25
- (C) 35
- (D) 59

7. There are 64 people standing in 8 lines. There is an equal number of people in each line.

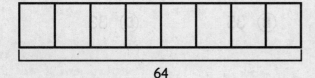

64

How many people are in each line?

- (A) 8
- (B) 70
- (C) 6
- (D) 9

8. Kate has 38 photos on her digital camera. She deletes 29 photos.

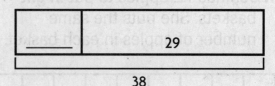

How many photos does she have left?

- (A) 19
- (C) 9
- (B) 67
- (D) 10

9. An array has 35 blocks. Each row has 7 blocks. How many rows are there?

- (A) 8
- (C) 4
- (B) 5
- (D) 28

10. A store displays 54 bananas in bunches of 6. How many bunches are there?

- (A) 7
- (C) 8
- (B) 10
- (D) 9

GO ON

11. Priya needs 6 beads to make a bracelet. She wants to make 10 bracelets. Beads come in packs of 5. How many packs of beads does Priya need?

Ⓐ 12 Ⓒ 60

Ⓑ 21 Ⓓ 30

12. Alexis has 118 tiger stickers and 208 lion stickers.

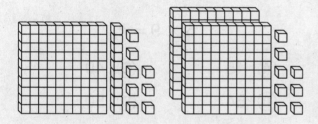

How many tiger and lion stickers does she have in all?

Ⓐ 336 Ⓒ 90

Ⓑ 325 Ⓓ 326

13. What is the missing number?

$$b \div 6 = 6$$

Ⓐ 6 Ⓒ 1

Ⓑ 36 Ⓓ 12

14. Stephanie has 52 pennies. Wil has 29 pennies. Stephanie gives 13 pennies away.

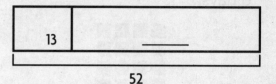

How many more pennies does Stephanie have than Wil now?

Ⓐ 39 Ⓒ 10

Ⓑ 36 Ⓓ 28

15. Each car on a train has 8 wheels. How many wheels do 7 train cars have?

Record your answer and fill in the bubbles on the grid. Be sure to use the correct place value.

⊙	⊙	⊙	.
⓪	⓪	⓪	
①	①	①	
②	②	②	
③	③	③	
④	④	④	
⑤	⑤	⑤	
⑥	⑥	⑥	
⑦	⑦	⑦	
⑧	⑧	⑧	
⑨	⑨	⑨	

GO ON

16. Aidan has 24 picture frames to paint. He wants to paint the same number of frames each day for 6 days.

How many frames does he need to paint each day?

(A) 3

(B) 18

(C) 4

(D) 8

17. There were 246 people at the zoo on Saturday and 370 people at the zoo on Sunday.

←——————————————→

How many people were at the zoo during the two days?

(A) 616

(B) 516

(C) 124

(D) 606

18. Andres has 40 small slices of watermelon. He gives the same number of slices to himself and 4 friends. Then he eats 2 of his slices. How many slices does he have left?

(A) 10   (C) 20

(B) 6   (D) 8

19. What is the missing number?

$$5 \times 9 = k$$

(A) 45   (C) 40

(B) 54   (D) 50

20. Evan takes $35 to camp. He divides his money into equal amounts for the 5 days he will be at camp. On the first day, he spends $3. How much money does he have left to spend on the first day?

(A) $11

(B) $3

(C) $7

(D) $4

GO ON

21. Grant made this number pattern. Which rule best describes the pattern.

56, 61, 66, 71, 76, ___

Ⓐ Add 4.

Ⓑ Add 5.

Ⓒ Subtract 4.

Ⓓ Subtract 5.

22. What is the unknown factor?

$42 \div \blacksquare = 7$

Record your answer and fill in the bubbles on the grid. Be sure to use the correct place value.

⓪	⓪	⓪	·
①	①	①	
②	②	②	
③	③	③	
④	④	④	
⑤	⑤	⑤	
⑥	⑥	⑥	
⑦	⑦	⑦	
⑧	⑧	⑧	
⑨	⑨	⑨	

23. Makayla has 64 crayons. Hattie has 38 crayons. Makayla gives 21 crayons to Sadie.

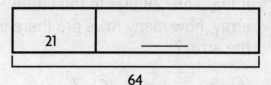

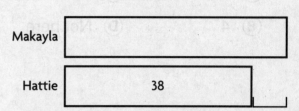

How many more crayons does Makayla have than Hattie now?

Ⓐ 43 Ⓑ 17 Ⓒ 38 Ⓓ 5

24. There are 134 chickens and 118 geese on a farm. How many chickens and geese are on the farm?

Ⓐ 252   Ⓒ 16

Ⓑ 242   Ⓓ 253

25. Carly and Jack each made a quilt with 36 squares. Carly made 6 rows with the same number in each row. Jack made 4 rows with the same number in each row. How many more squares are in each of Jack's rows than each of Carly's rows?

Ⓐ 6 Ⓑ 3 Ⓒ 9 Ⓓ 2

GO ON

26. The first row of an array is shown.

■ ■ ■ ■

If there are 28 tiles in the entire array, how many rows are there in the array?

(A) 5   (C) 7

(B) 4   (D) Not here

27. Kathleen buys 7 bags of oranges for a picnic. There are 8 oranges in each bag.

| 8 | 8 | 8 | 8 | 8 | 8 | 8 |

_____

How many oranges does she buy?

(A) 56   (C) 15

(B) 48   (D) 64

28. Rebecca bought 48 hamburger buns for a party. The buns come in packages of 8. How many packages did she buy?

(A) 5   (C) 8

(B) 6   (D) 7

29. The table shows the number of points scored in a game.

Round	Molly	Jason
1	21	20
2	20	18
3	19	19
4	16	26

In which round did Molly and Jason score the most points together?

(A) Round 4

(B) Round 3

(C) Round 2

(D) Round 1

30. Charles put 86 jelly beans in a jar. Fifty-eight of them are green. The rest are yellow. How many are yellow?

(A) 32

(B) 144

(C) 29

(D) 28

STOP

Fill in the bubble for the correct answer.

1. Ryan uses pattern blocks to make a design. Then he sorts the pattern blocks in a Venn diagram. The circles are labeled "Quadrilaterals" and "Polygons with Right Angles."

   Where should he place the square in the Venn diagram?

   Ⓐ in "Quadrilaterals"

   Ⓑ in "Polygons with Right Angles"

   Ⓒ in the section where the circles overlap

   Ⓓ outside both circles

2. Which solid shape has 6 faces?

   Ⓐ

   Ⓑ

   Ⓒ

   Ⓓ

3. Sam drew these quadrilaterals.

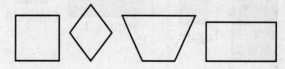

   How many rhombuses did he draw?

   Ⓐ 1   Ⓑ 4   Ⓒ 2   Ⓓ 3

4. What is the name of this three-dimensional solid?

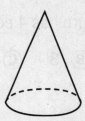

   Ⓐ cone   Ⓒ cube

   Ⓑ sphere   Ⓓ cylinder

5. Zach draws a quadrilateral that has 4 right angles. Each of the pairs of opposite sides are parallel. There are two different lengths of sides, but the opposite sides have the same length. What type of quadrilateral is it?

   Ⓐ rectangle   Ⓒ rhombus

   Ⓑ trapezoid   Ⓓ square

   GO ON ➡

Use the shapes for 6–7.

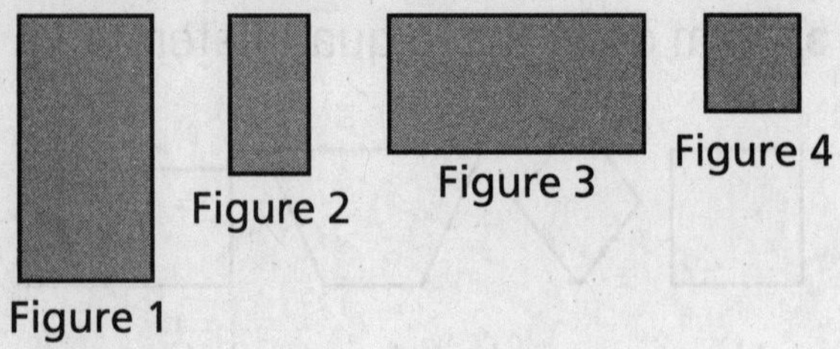

Figure 4

Figure 2

Figure 3

Figure 1

6. Which two figures appear to be congruent?

Ⓐ 1 and 2   Ⓒ 3 and 4

Ⓑ 1 and 3   Ⓓ 2 and 4

7. Which figure has 4 equal sides?

Ⓐ 1   Ⓑ 3   Ⓒ 2   Ⓓ 4

8. If Olivia connects points A and B, what quadrilateral will she draw?

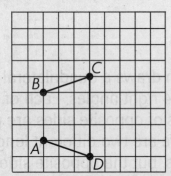

Ⓐ parallelogram   Ⓒ rhombus

Ⓑ trapezoid   Ⓓ square

9. Nicholas received a package in this box.

Which three-dimensional solid is the box shaped like?

Ⓐ triangular prism

Ⓑ rectangular prism

Ⓒ cylinder

Ⓓ sphere

10. Alexa drew these polygons. Which is **NOT** a trapezoid?

Ⓐ

Ⓑ

Ⓒ

Ⓓ

GO ON ➡

11. Adriana draws a trapezoid. How many pairs of opposite sides are parallel in the trapezoid?

Record your answer and fill in the bubbles on the grid. Be sure to use the correct place value.

⓪	⓪	⓪	·
①	①	①	
②	②	②	
③	③	③	
④	④	④	
⑤	⑤	⑤	
⑥	⑥	⑥	
⑦	⑦	⑦	
⑧	⑧	⑧	
⑨	⑨	⑨	

12. Ellie drew a quadrilateral that is **NOT** a parallelogram. Which shape did she draw?

Ⓐ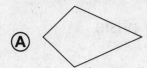

Ⓑ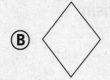

Ⓒ

Ⓓ

13. Lucas wound some yarn.

Which three-dimensional solid is the yarn shaped like?

Ⓐ cube   Ⓒ cylinder

Ⓑ sphere   Ⓓ cone

Use the quadrilateral for 14–15.

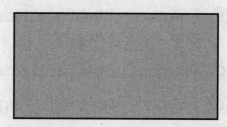

14. Which pattern blocks can you combine to make a shape that is congruent to the quadrilateral?

Ⓐ 2 squares   Ⓒ 2 trapezoids

Ⓑ 2 cubes   Ⓓ 2 hexagons

15. How many right angles does the quadrilateral have?

Ⓐ 1

Ⓑ 3

Ⓒ 2

Ⓓ 4

GO ON

16. What label could describe only the figures in the section where the circles overlap?

- (A) Rectangles
- (B) Polygons with 4 Equal Sides and 4 Right Angles
- (C) Polygons with 4 Equal Sides
- (D) Polygons with 4 Right Angles

17. Savannah stacked blocks for her baby sister. Which three-dimensional solids did she use for this tower?

- (A) a cylinder and a cone
- (B) a rectangular prism and a cube
- (C) a cone and a triangular prism
- (D) sphere and a cylinder

18. Jonah has a block shaped like this figure.

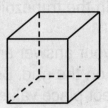

What shape is this block?

- (A) cone
- (C) sphere
- (B) cylinder
- (D) cube

Use the three-dimensional solid for 19–20.

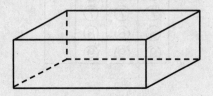

19. What is the name of the three-dimensional solid?

- (A) triangular prism
- (B) sphere
- (C) rectangular prism
- (D) cube

20. How many vertices does the three-dimensional solid have?

- (A) 4
- (B) 8
- (C) 6
- (D) 2

Fill in the bubble for the correct answer.

1. Abby is drawing a sketch for a flower garden. Each unit square is 1 square foot.

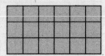

Which multiplication equation can be used to find the area of the flower garden?

Ⓐ $6 + 3 = 9$

Ⓑ $6 \times 6 = 36$

Ⓒ $3 \times 3 = 9$

Ⓓ $3 \times 6 = 18$

2. Tim made a drawing of his hallway. Each unit square is 1 square foot.

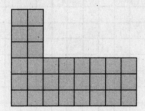

What is the area of their hallway?

Ⓐ 24 square feet

Ⓑ 30 square feet

Ⓒ 12 square feet

Ⓓ 18 square feet

3. Mrs. Lopez divides her lawn into 8 rectangles of the same size. If she mows one rectangle, what fraction of the lawn does she mow?

Ⓐ $\frac{1}{8}$

Ⓑ $\frac{1}{6}$

Ⓒ $\frac{1}{6}$

Ⓓ $\frac{1}{4}$

4. William made a cloth napkin by sewing together 1-inch squares.

What is the area of the napkin?

Ⓐ 16 square inches

Ⓑ 14 square inches

Ⓒ 12 square inches

Ⓓ 10 square inches

GO ON

5. Isabella has a red rug that is 2 feet wide and 4 feet long. She has a blue rug that is 4 feet wide and 8 feet long. How are the areas of the rugs different?

Ⓐ The area of the blue rug is 4 times as large as the area of the red rug.

Ⓑ The area of the blue rug is 8 times as large as the area of the red rug.

Ⓒ The area of the red rug is 4 times as large as the area of the blue rug.

Ⓓ The area of the red rug is 8 times as large as the area of the blue rug.

6. Victor is cutting out 8 squares of equal size for a blanket. If he has cut out one square of the blanket, what fraction of the blanket has he cut out?

Ⓐ $\frac{1}{4}$

Ⓑ $\frac{1}{3}$

Ⓒ $\frac{1}{8}$

Ⓓ $\frac{1}{6}$

7. Claire draws a design with chalk on paper. She uses 1-inch squares.

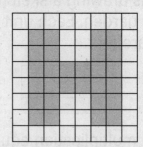

What is the area of her design?

Ⓐ 24 square inches

Ⓑ 12 square inches

Ⓒ 28 square inches

Ⓓ 26 square inches

8. Daniel painted this design.

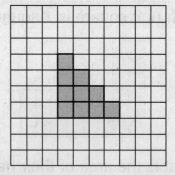

If each unit square is one square foot, how many square feet did he paint?

Ⓐ 7 square feet

Ⓑ 8 square feet

Ⓒ 12 square feet

Ⓓ 10 square feet

GO ON ➡

9. Julie divided this rectangle into 4 parts with equal areas. What is the area of each part?

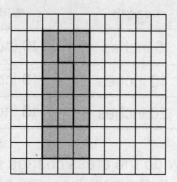

   (A) 4 square units

   (B) 6 square units

   (C) 5 square units

   (D) 3 square units

10. Kevin shades squares for an art project. Each unit is 1 square inch. How many more square inches of light gray does he shade than square inches of dark gray?

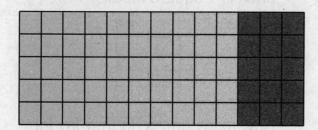

   (A) 35   (C) 65

   (B) 25   (D) 55

11. Marcus drew this rectangle.

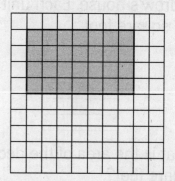

Which multiplication sentence can be used to find the area of the rectangle?

   (A) $4 + 4 + 4 + 4 = 16$

   (B) $7 \times 7 = 49$

   (C) $7 \times 4 = 28$

   (D) $4 \times 4 = 16$

12. Diana divided this rectangle into 5 parts with equal area. What is the area of each part?

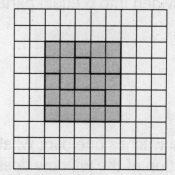

   (A) 4 square units

   (B) 5 square units

   (C) 3 square units

   (D) 6 square units

   GO ON ➡

13. The diagram shows the deck at Andrew's house. Each unit square is 1 square foot.

What is the area of the deck in square feet?

Record your answer and fill in the bubbles on the grid. Be sure to use the correct place value.

14. Jonathan is washing a window that is divided into 6 equal parts.

If he washes one part, what fraction of the window does he wash?

Ⓐ $\frac{1}{6}$ Ⓑ $\frac{1}{3}$ Ⓒ $\frac{1}{4}$ Ⓓ $\frac{1}{8}$

15. David frames three pictures shown in the table.

Length	Width
5 inches	10 inches
10 inches	10 inches
20 inches	10 inches

How do the areas change from one row to the next?

Ⓐ The areas do not change.

Ⓑ The areas double.

Ⓒ The areas increase by 50 square inches.

Ⓓ The areas increase by 100 square inches.

16. Eliza is helping her parents lay bricks for a new walkway. Each brick is 1 square meter.

How many bricks do they lay for the new walkway?

Ⓐ 12   Ⓒ 9

Ⓑ 11   Ⓓ 10

STOP

Name _____

Fill in the bubble for the correct answer.

1. Alex is sewing fabric around the edge of a rectangular quilt. The quilt has side lengths of 4 feet and 5 feet. How many feet of fabric will Alex need for the quilt?

   (A) 1 foot   (C) 45 feet

   (B) 9 feet   (D) 18 feet

2. Eddie modeled a shape on a geoboard.

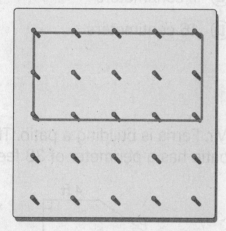

   What is the perimeter of the shape?

   (A) 14 units   (C) 6 units

   (B) 12 units   (D) 10 units

3. Kylie makes a triangular picture frame. What is the perimeter of the frame if each side is 5 inches?

   (A) 15 inches   (C) 14 inches

   (B) 10 inches   (D) 18 inches

4. Jasmine designs a six-sided dog run in her backyard. The perimeter is 36 meters.

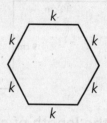

   How long will each side be?

   (A) 6 meters

   (B) 4 meters

   (C) 9 meters

   (D) 5 meters

5. Katy cuts some paper squares for an art project.

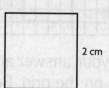

   What is the perimeter of each paper square?

   (A) 4 centimeters

   (B) 2 centimeters

   (C) 10 centimeters

   (D) 8 centimeters

GO ON

6. The perimeter of this shape is
48 centimeters.

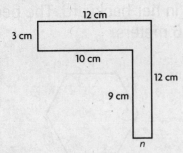

What is the length of side *n*?

Ⓐ 4 centimeters

Ⓑ 3 centimeters

Ⓒ 2 centimeters

Ⓓ 12 centimeters

7. What is the perimeter of the
rectangle in units?

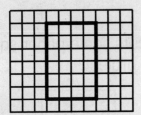

Record your answer and fill in the
bubbles on the grid. Be sure to use
the correct place value.

⓪	⓪	⓪	.
①	①	①	
②	②	②	
③	③	③	
④	④	④	
⑤	⑤	⑤	
⑥	⑥	⑥	
⑦	⑦	⑦	
⑧	⑧	⑧	
⑨	⑨	⑨	

8. Benjamin paints a green rectangle
in a mural.

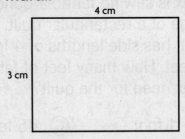

What is the perimeter of the
rectangle?

Ⓐ 21 centimeters

Ⓑ 14 centimeters

Ⓒ 7 centimeters

Ⓓ 16 centimeters

9. Mr. Ferris is building a patio. The
patio has a perimeter of 33 feet.

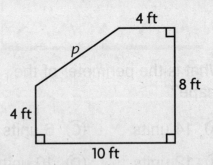

What is the length of the unknown
side?

Ⓐ 10 feet

Ⓑ 6 feet

Ⓒ 7 feet

Ⓓ 9 feet

GO ON

10. A swimming pool has this shape.

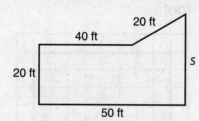

The perimeter of the pool is 160 feet. What is the length of the unknown side?

(A) 50 feet   (C) 40 feet

(B) 30 feet   (D) 20 feet

11. Lydia measured the sides of a stop sign. Each side is 12 inches.

What is the perimeter of the sign?

(A) 84 inches   (C) 48 inches

(B) 72 inches   (D) 96 inches

12. A square playground has a side length of 62 feet. What is the perimeter of the playground?

(A) 124 feet   (C) 248 feet

(B) 242 feet   (D) 186 feet

13. Jonah drew a shape. Its perimeter is 11 centimeters.

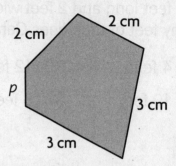

What is the length of the unknown side?

(A) 1 centimeter

(B) 3 centimeters

(C) 2 centimeters

(D) 4 centimeters

14. Natalia draws a shape on grid paper.

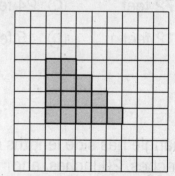

What is the perimeter of the shape?

(A) 18 units   (C) 17 units

(B) 13 units   (D) 19 units

GO ON

15. Cara puts tape around the edges of a poster. The rectangular poster is 3 feet long and 2 feet wide. How many feet of tape does Cara need?

Ⓐ 4 feet   Ⓒ 12 feet

Ⓑ 10 feet   Ⓓ 5 feet

16. Bella's vegetable garden has a perimeter of 72 feet.

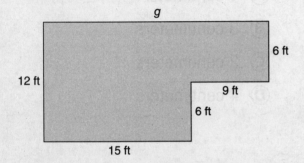

What is the length of the unknown side?

Ⓐ 72 feet   Ⓒ 24 feet

Ⓑ 12 feet   Ⓓ 15 feet

17. A triangle has side lengths of 20 inches, 20 inches, and 24 inches. What is the perimeter of the triangle?

Ⓐ 84 inches   Ⓒ 62 inches

Ⓑ 44 inches   Ⓓ 64 inches

18. Tess is designing a patio. Each unit is 1 foot.

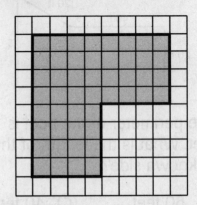

What is the perimeter of the patio?

Ⓐ 16 feet   Ⓒ 28 feet

Ⓑ 32 feet   Ⓓ 24 feet

19. George cut out a paper triangle to paste on a poster.

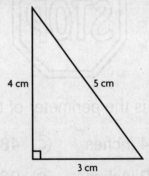

What is the perimeter of the triangle?

Ⓐ 13 centimeters

Ⓑ 12 centimeters

Ⓒ 14 centimeters

Ⓓ 11 centimeters

STOP

Fill in the bubble for the correct answer.

1. Jake has swimming practice from 4:10 P.M. to 4:50 P.M. He stretches for 10 minutes and practices turns for 8 minutes. He spends the rest of the time swimming laps. How much time does Jake spend swimming laps?

   (A) 22 minutes   (C) 18 minutes

   (B) 28 minutes   (D) 40 minutes

2. Eva needs 2 quarts of water to make lemonade. How many pints of water does she need?

   (A) 2 pints   (C) 1 pint

   (B) 4 pints   (D) 8 pints

3. Ellie spends from 7:07 A.M. to 7:35 A.M. eating breakfast. How many minutes does it take her to eat breakfast?

   (A) 28 minutes   (C) 42 minutes

   (B) 32 minutes   (D) 25 minutes

4. Which fraction names the point closest to 0 on the number line?

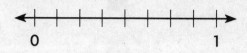

   0   1

   (A) $\frac{1}{2}$

   (B) $\frac{7}{8}$

   (C) $\frac{5}{8}$

   (D) $\frac{3}{4}$

5. Melanie works at a zoo. She feeds the giraffes at 4:35 P.M. She feeds the elephants 30 minutes after that. At what time does she feed the elephants?

   (A) 4:05 P.M.

   (B) 5:10 P.M.

   (C) 5:45 P.M.

   (D) 5:05 P.M.

GO ON

6. Which measurement unit should be used for the liquid volume of the container?

Ⓐ liters

Ⓑ pounds

Ⓒ inches

Ⓓ grams

7. A small bag of apples weighs about 20 ounces. Which item would be about the same weight as the bag of apples?

Ⓐ 4 pieces of chewing gum

Ⓑ 1 slice of bread

Ⓒ 1 basketball

Ⓓ 1 ball of yarn

8. Dana practices piano from 3:32 P.M. to 3:55 P.M. How much time does Dana spend practicing piano?

Ⓐ 33 minutes

Ⓑ 87 minutes

Ⓒ 25 minutes

Ⓓ 23 minutes

9. Fred gets to school at 8:25 A.M. He walked for 5 minutes to the bus stop and his bus ride was 30 minutes. What time did Fred leave home?

Ⓐ 7:55 A.M.   Ⓒ 8:30 A.M.

Ⓑ 8:00 A.M.   Ⓓ 7:50 A.M.

10. Which unit would be best to measure the mass of a bowling ball?

Ⓐ kilograms

Ⓑ grams

Ⓒ ounces

Ⓓ liters

GO ON

11. Which fraction names the point closest to 0 on the number line?

Ⓐ $\frac{3}{4}$

Ⓑ $\frac{2}{4}$

Ⓒ $\frac{5}{8}$

Ⓓ $\frac{7}{8}$

12. Trace starts soccer practice at 3:30 P.M. Molly starts soccer practice 45 minutes later. At what time does Molly start soccer practice?

Ⓐ 2:45 P.M. Ⓒ 4:15 P.M.

Ⓑ 3:45 P.M. Ⓓ 3:15 P.M.

13. Liza is pouring pizza sauce onto a pizza crust. Which amount of pizza sauce is reasonable for one pizza?

Ⓐ 4 quarts

Ⓑ 1 cup

Ⓒ 1 gallon

Ⓓ 4 pints

14. Jorge buys 6 packages of hot dog buns for a picnic. Each package weighs about 8 ounces. About how many pounds do the hot dog buns weigh in all?

Record your answer and fill in the bubbles on the grid. Be sure to use the correct place value.

⓪	⓪	⓪	
①	①	①	
②	②	②	
③	③	③	
④	④	④	
⑤	⑤	⑤	
⑥	⑥	⑥	
⑦	⑦	⑦	
⑧	⑧	⑧	
⑨	⑨	⑨	

15. Arianna spends 15 minutes eating a snack and 40 minutes doing her homework after school. She finishes at 4:40 P.M. At what time does she start?

Ⓐ 3:45 P.M.

Ⓑ 4:05 P.M.

Ⓒ 5:20 P.M.

Ⓓ 4:55 P.M.

GO ON

16. Which unit should be used to measure the capacity of the container?

Ⓐ quart

Ⓑ gallon

Ⓒ cup

Ⓓ pint

17. Which fraction names the point farthest from 0 on the number line?

Ⓐ $\frac{1}{2}$

Ⓑ $\frac{1}{4}$

Ⓒ $\frac{3}{4}$

Ⓓ $\frac{7}{8}$

18. Martha placed a rock on one side of a balance.

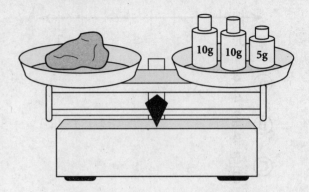

What is the mass of the rock?

Ⓐ 3 grams Ⓒ 3 kilograms

Ⓑ 25 grams Ⓓ 25 kilograms

19. Kevin sets the table 30 minutes before dinner is served. Dinner is served at 6:15 P.M. At what time does Kevin set the table?

Ⓐ 6:45 P.M. Ⓒ 7:15 P.M.

Ⓑ 5:45 P.M. Ⓓ 6:00 P.M.

20. Which container has more than 1 liter of liquid volume when it is filled?

Ⓐ a drinking glass

Ⓑ a yogurt container

Ⓒ a teacup

Ⓓ a kids' swimming pool

Fill in the bubble for the correct answer.

1. Which measurement unit should be used to find the liquid volume of the container?

Ⓐ grams   Ⓒ cups

Ⓑ pounds   Ⓓ liters

2. Ally cuts out a pentagon to make a sign for her door. The perimeter is 30 inches.

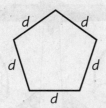

How long is each side?

Ⓐ 180 inches   Ⓒ 4 inches

Ⓑ 6 inches   Ⓓ 5 inches

3. Kevin has an art class at 3:10 P.M. He has a music class 45 minutes after his art class starts. At what time does he have a music class?

Ⓐ 3:55 P.M.   Ⓒ 2:25 P.M.

Ⓑ 3:40 P.M.   Ⓓ 3:45 P.M.

4. Diana divided a rectangle into 5 parts that have equal area. What is the area of each part?

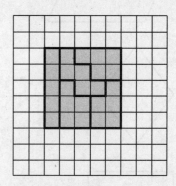

Ⓐ 4 square units

Ⓑ 7 square units

Ⓒ 5 square units

Ⓓ 6 square units

5. Jenna drew a design on grid paper.

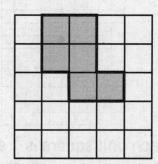

What is the perimeter of the design?

Ⓐ 13 units   Ⓒ 9 units

Ⓑ 12 units   Ⓓ 11 units

GO ON ➡

6. Connor drew 4 figures. Which figure is a trapezoid?

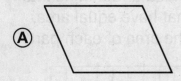

Ⓐ

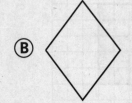

Ⓑ

Ⓒ

Ⓓ

7. Esteban drew a sketch of the cover for the community swimming pool in his town.

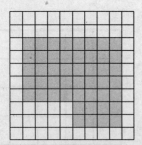

If each unit square is 1 square meter, how many square meters is the cover for the swimming pool?

Ⓐ 53 square meters

Ⓑ 30 square meters

Ⓒ 48 square meters

Ⓓ 40 square meters

8. Which fraction names the point farthest from 0 on the number line?

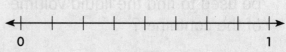

Ⓐ $\frac{1}{8}$

Ⓑ $\frac{1}{2}$

Ⓒ $\frac{7}{8}$

Ⓓ $\frac{2}{8}$

9. Gabriela placed a strawberry on one side of a balance.

What is the mass of the strawberry?

Ⓐ 12 grams

Ⓑ 2 grams

Ⓒ 12 kilograms

Ⓓ 2 kilograms

GO ON

10. Julian is unfolding a tablecloth. It starts as a square with a length of 1 foot on each side. He unfolds it so it is 2 feet on each side. Then he unfolds it again so it is 4 feet on each side. How does the area of the visible part of the folded tablecloth change as Julian unfolds it?

(A) It stays the same.

(B) It doubles.

(C) It is 3 times the area of the one before.

(D) It is 4 times the area of the one before.

11. Luke cut out a square to make a patch for his jacket.

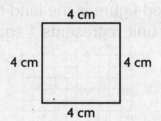

What is the perimeter of the square?

(A) 15 centimeters

(B) 16 centimeters

(C) 12 centimeters

(D) 8 centimeters

12. Makayla spends 10 minutes making a sandwich and 30 minutes eating her lunch. She finishes at 12:55 P.M. At what time does she start?

(A) 12:20 P.M.

(B) 12:15 P.M.

(C) 12:30 P.M.

(D) 12:10 P.M.

13. Kareem makes a rectangle out of connected tiles.

What is the area, in tiles, of the rectangle?

Record your answer and fill in the bubbles on the grid. Be sure to use the correct place value.

⓪	⓪	⓪	.
①	①	①	
②	②	②	
③	③	③	
④	④	④	
⑤	⑤	⑤	
⑥	⑥	⑥	
⑦	⑦	⑦	
⑧	⑧	⑧	
⑨	⑨	⑨	

GO ON ➡

14. Which two figures appear to be congruent?

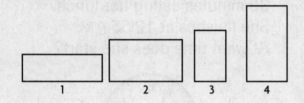

1   2   3   4

Ⓐ 1 and 2   Ⓒ 3 and 4

Ⓑ 1 and 3   Ⓓ 2 and 4

15. Alex notices a quadrilateral in a mosaic picture. It has 4 equal sides, but no right angles. What type of quadrilateral is it?

Ⓐ rhombus

Ⓑ trapezoid

Ⓒ rectangle

Ⓓ square

16. Which unit should be used to measure the capacity of the container?

Ⓐ quart   Ⓒ cup

Ⓑ gallon   Ⓓ pint

17. What label could describe the figures in the circle on the left?

Ⓐ Squares   Ⓒ Rectangles

Ⓑ Trapezoids   Ⓓ Rhombuses

18. Elizabeth's deck is a rectangle that is 12 feet long and 15 feet wide. What is the perimeter of the deck?

Ⓐ 27 feet   Ⓒ 54 feet

Ⓑ 50 feet   Ⓓ 36 feet

19. Eric is playing a board game. The shaded figure is the land he owns. Each unit represents 1 square mile.

How many square miles of land does Eric own in the game?

Ⓐ 28 square miles

Ⓑ 12 square miles

Ⓒ 7 square miles

Ⓓ 14 square miles

GO ON ➡

20. Joe picks up 8 books. Each book weighs about 8 ounces. About how many pounds do the books weigh in all?

Ⓐ 5 pounds   Ⓒ 8 pounds

Ⓑ 2 pounds   Ⓓ 4 pounds

23. Maddie starts school at 8:05 A.M. Her brother Blake starts school 45 minutes later. What time does Blake start school?

Ⓐ 8:50 A.M.   Ⓒ 7:20 A.M.

Ⓑ 8:15 A.M.   Ⓓ 8:45 A.M.

21. Which three-dimensional solid is shaped like a basketball?

Ⓐ sphere   Ⓒ cube

Ⓑ cylinder   Ⓓ cone

24. Which fraction is closest to 0 on the number line?

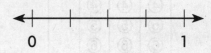

0 ⊢———⊣———⊣———⊣———⊣ 1

Ⓐ $\frac{2}{4}$ Ⓒ $\frac{4}{4}$

Ⓑ $\frac{1}{4}$ Ⓓ $\frac{3}{4}$

22. Evan shaded a grid to show the size of a maze he is building for his hamster. Each unit square is 1 square inch.

How many square inches will the maze be?

Ⓐ 16 square inches

Ⓑ 25 square inches

Ⓒ 41 square inches

Ⓓ 38 square inches

25. Delia cut a strip from a piece of fabric. Each square unit is 1 square inch.

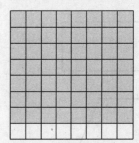

What fraction of the fabric does she cut off?

Ⓐ $\frac{1}{6}$ Ⓒ $\frac{1}{2}$

Ⓑ $\frac{1}{4}$ Ⓓ $\frac{1}{8}$

GO ON ➡

26. Logan draws a rectangle. How many pairs of opposite sides are parallel in the rectangle?

Record your answer and fill in the bubbles on the grid. Be sure to use the correct place value.

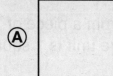

27. Megan drew these shapes. Which one is **NOT** a parallelogram?

Ⓐ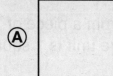

Ⓑ

Ⓒ

Ⓓ

28. Victor mixes 1 quart of white milk and 1 quart of chocolate milk. How many cups of milk does he have?

Ⓐ 4 cups Ⓒ 7 cups

Ⓑ 16 cups Ⓓ Not here

29. Which container has less than 1 liter of liquid volume when it is filled?

Ⓐ a tea cup

Ⓑ a kitchen sink

Ⓒ a barrel

Ⓓ a large bird bath

30. Antonio measured the perimeter of his garden. The perimeter of the garden is 14 feet.

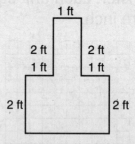

What is the length of the unknown side?

Ⓐ 3 feet Ⓒ 4 feet

Ⓑ 1 foot Ⓓ 2 feet

Name _____

Fill in the bubble for the correct answer.

Use the pictograph for 1–2.

Favorite Colors

Color	Votes
Red	✎✎✎✎✎✎✎✎
Blue	✎✎✎✎✎
Purple	✎✎✎✎✎✎✎✎✎
Green	✎✎✎
Yellow	✎✎✎✎✎✎

1. How many people chose blue as their favorite color?

Ⓐ 11

Ⓑ 10

Ⓒ 7

Ⓓ 5

2. How many more people chose purple than green as their favorite color?

Ⓐ 11

Ⓑ 6

Ⓒ 8

Ⓓ 5

Use the dot plot for 3–5.

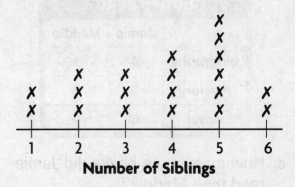

Number of Siblings

3. How many people surveyed have more than 4 brothers and sisters?

Ⓐ 12   Ⓒ 4

Ⓑ 8   Ⓓ 7

4. How many people surveyed have only one brother or one sister?

Ⓐ 2   Ⓒ 3

Ⓑ 4   Ⓓ 1

5. How many more people have 5 or 6 brothers and sisters than 3 or 4?

Ⓐ 2   Ⓒ 1

Ⓑ 3   Ⓓ 15

GO ON

Use the frequency table for 6–7.

Books Read

	Jamie	Maddie
biography	4	1
mystery	6	3
novel	6	9

6. How many more books did Jamie read than Maddie?

- (A) 16
- (B) 8
- (C) 3
- (D) 2

7. How many mysteries did Jamie read?

- (A) 6
- (B) 3
- (C) 4
- (D) 9

Use the pictograph for 8–9.

Favorite Outside Activities for Mr. Metz's Third Grade Class

Tennis	☼ ☼ ◗
Swimming	☼ ☼ ☼ ☼
Golfing	☼ ◗
Biking	☼ ☼ ☼ ◗
Hiking	☼ ☼ ☼

Each ☼ stands for 2.

8. How many more students chose swimming than golfing?

- (A) 2
- (B) 5
- (C) 3
- (D) 1

9. How many students chose an activity?

- (A) 29
- (B) 30
- (C) 28
- (D) 26

GO ON

Name _____

Use the bar graph for 10–11.

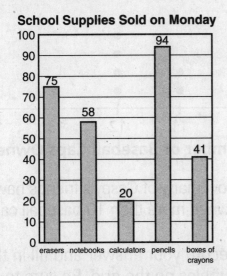

Use the dot plot for 12–13.

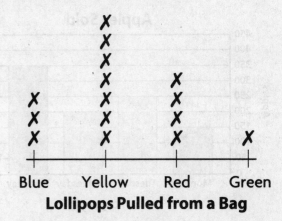

Lollipops Pulled from a Bag

10. The bar graph shows the number of school supplies sold at a store on Monday. The store also sold markers. At what number on the scale would a bar for markers end if the store sold the same number of markers as calculators?

Record your answer and fill in the bubbles on the grid. Be sure to use the correct place value.

11. How many more erasers than calculators and boxes of crayons were sold?

Ⓐ 34 Ⓑ 14 Ⓒ 55 Ⓓ 15

12. How many more yellow and red lollipops than blue and green lollipops were pulled out of the bag?

Ⓐ 7
Ⓑ 3
Ⓒ 4
Ⓓ 6

13. How many red lollipops were pulled out of the bag?

Ⓐ 1
Ⓑ 7
Ⓒ 4
Ⓓ 3

GO ON

Use the bar graph for 14–15.

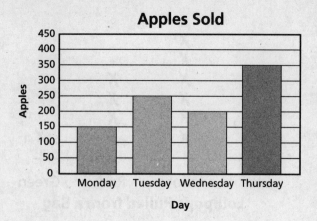

Use the dot plot for 16–17.

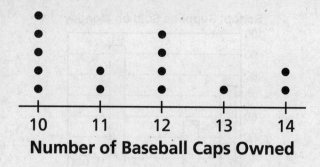

Number of Baseball Caps Owned

14. How many apples were sold on Wednesday?

Ⓐ 150

Ⓑ 250

Ⓒ 200

Ⓓ 350

16. How many of Casey's friends have owned more than 10 baseball caps?

Record your answer and fill in the bubbles on the grid. Be sure to use the correct place value.

⓪	⓪	⓪	.
①	①	①	
②	②	②	
③	③	③	
④	④	④	
⑤	⑤	⑤	
⑥	⑥	⑥	
⑦	⑦	⑦	
⑧	⑧	⑧	
⑨	⑨	⑨	

15. How many apples were sold in all?

Ⓐ 950

Ⓑ 850

Ⓒ 900

Ⓓ 750

17. How would you change the dot plot if 3 more people each owned 13 baseball caps?

Ⓐ Draw three more dots above 12.

Ⓑ Draw two more dots above 13.

Ⓒ Draw three more dots above 13.

Ⓓ Draw two more dots above 14.

GO ON

Name _____

Use the bar graph for 18–19.

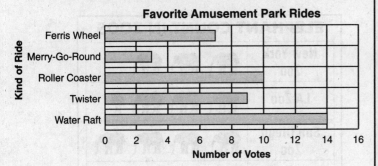

Favorite Amusement Park Rides

18. How many people chose merry-go-round?

(A) 5

(B) 4

(C) 1

(D) 3

19. How many fewer chose Ferris wheel than roller coaster and water raft combined?

(A) 17

(B) 7

(C) 3

(D) 15

Use the frequency table for 20–21.

Rainfall in Kylie's Town	
Month	Number of Inches
April	6
May	7
June	4

20. How many inches of rain fell in Kylie's town in the three months?

(A) 17 inches

(B) 13 inches

(C) 15 inches

(D) 11 inches

21. How many inches of rain fell in Kylie's town in May?

(A) 6

(B) 4

(C) 7

(D) Not here

GO ON

Name _____

Use the frequency table for 22–23.

Tents Sold
Week 1: 卌
Week 2: 卌 卌 ll
Week 3: 卌 ll
Week 4: 卌 卌

22. In which week were the most tents sold?

Ⓐ Week 1

Ⓑ Week 2

Ⓒ Week 3

Ⓓ Week 4

23. How many fewer tents were sold in Week 1 than in Weeks 2 and 3 combined?

Ⓐ 14

Ⓑ 7

Ⓒ 19

Ⓓ 5

Use the pictograph for 24–25.

ELEPHANT COUNT IN ZOOS

New York Zoo	
LA Zoo	
San Diego Zoo	
Washington Zoo	

Each 🐘 = 12 elephants.

24. Which zoo has 42 elephants?

Ⓐ New York Zoo

Ⓑ LA Zoo

Ⓒ San Diego Zoo

Ⓓ Washington Zoo

25. How many elephants are at the LA Zoo and the San Diego Zoo altogether?

Ⓐ 84

Ⓑ 48

Ⓒ 8

Ⓓ 90

STOP

Fill in the bubble for the correct answer.

1. Matthew plans to spend $65 for a new skateboard. He has $25 and plans to save $10 each week. If he does not make any unplanned purchases, how many weeks will he need to save to have enough money to purchase the skateboard?

   Ⓐ 6

   Ⓑ 4

   Ⓒ 5

   Ⓓ 40

2. Trinity made a savings plan to help her save money for an MP3 player that costs $55. How many months does she need to save so she can buy the player?

Month	1	2	3	4	5
Amount Saved	$15	$30	$45	$60	$75

   Ⓐ 5

   Ⓑ 1

   Ⓒ 4

   Ⓓ 3

3. Malia earns $5 per hour raking leaves. She puts all of the money she earns in her bank account. Which best describes what she does with her money?

   Ⓐ saving   Ⓒ credit

   Ⓑ spending   Ⓓ giving

4. Eve likes stuffed animals. For every 2 hours she spends helping her father in the garden, she earns one small stuffed animal. How many stuffed animals will she earn for 8 hours of working in the garden?

   Ⓐ 6   Ⓒ 8

   Ⓑ 16   Ⓓ 4

5. Tristan needs to buy 3 books for a class. Each book costs $10, but he has only saved $14. He borrows the rest of the money from his sister and pays her back $8 a week from his allowance. How many weeks will it take him to pay back his sister?

   Ⓐ 4   Ⓒ 2

   Ⓑ 3   Ⓓ 1

GO ON

6. Leslie earns $8 per hour selling passes to the pool. How much money does she earn if she works 8 hours?

Record your answer and fill in the bubbles on the grid. Be sure to use the correct place value.

			.
⓪	⓪	⓪	
①	①	①	
②	②	②	
③	③	③	
④	④	④	
⑤	⑤	⑤	
⑥	⑥	⑥	
⑦	⑦	⑦	
⑧	⑧	⑧	
⑨	⑨	⑨	

7. Elizabeth donated $30 to her school for school supplies. Which best describes her donation?

Ⓐ giving   Ⓒ income

Ⓑ saving   Ⓓ credit

8. Isaac takes a job earning $7 an hour. Which best describes the money he earns?

Ⓐ spending   Ⓒ income

Ⓑ saving   Ⓓ credit

9. Samantha wants to purchase a new jacket that costs $57. She has $64. If she makes an unplanned purchase of a book for $12, how much more money will she need before she can buy the jacket?

Ⓐ $7

Ⓑ $5

Ⓒ $12

Ⓓ $52

10. Which of the following is a true statement about a savings plan?

Ⓐ It will make sure you only buy things you need.

Ⓑ It will prevent you from buying things you do not need.

Ⓒ It will help you decide what item to buy.

Ⓓ It can help you pay for education.

GO ON

11. Kevin walks his neighbor's dog for $5 a week. Which best describes the money he receives?

Ⓐ spending   Ⓒ giving

Ⓑ credit   Ⓓ income

12. Elliot has a savings plan. He plans to save $15 each month. How much money will he have saved after 6 months?

Record your answer and fill in the bubbles on the grid. Be sure to use the correct place value.

Ⓞ	Ⓞ	Ⓞ	.
①	①	①	
②	②	②	
③	③	③	
④	④	④	
⑤	⑤	⑤	
⑥	⑥	⑥	
⑦	⑦	⑦	
⑧	⑧	⑧	
⑨	⑨	⑨	

13. Coach Clark needs to buy 4 soccer balls. He does not have enough money, so he borrows some money. What does he use to buy the soccer balls?

Ⓐ income   Ⓒ spending

Ⓑ credit   Ⓓ giving

14. A company makes T-shirts in different colors. When there are more shirts available, the cost is lower. The table shows the number of each color T-shirt they make every week.

T-shirts Made Each Week	
Colors	**Number Made**
Red	289
Blue	418
Green	358
Yellow	188

Which color of shirt most likely costs the most?

Ⓐ red   Ⓒ green

Ⓑ blue   Ⓓ yellow

15. Lila is saving money to buy dog food for an animal shelter. Which of the following best describes Lila's reason to save money?

Ⓐ to replace a broken item

Ⓑ to do something fun

Ⓒ to buy an item she wants

Ⓓ to help others

GO ON

16. Karin has saved $20. Next week, she will earn $15 helping her neighbor clean her garage. She wants to purchase a pair of shoes that costs $32. How much can Karin spend today if she plans to buy the shoes next week?

(A) $2   (C) $3

(B) $37   (D) $32

17. Nicholas borrowed $150 to pay for new sports equipment. Which best describes how he got the money?

(A) giving   (C) spending

(B) credit   (D) income

18. Madison would like to purchase a wheel for her hamster that costs $8. She saves $2 each week for 3 weeks. Then Madison spends $4 on trading cards. How many more weeks will Madison need to save to have enough money to buy the wheel?

(A) 1   (C) 4

(B) 3   (D) 2

19. Alyssa needs to buy 2 pairs of shorts for soccer. Each pair of shorts costs $8, but she has only $10 saved. She borrows the rest of the money from her mother. Alyssa will pay her mother back $2 a week. How many weeks will it take Alyssa to pay back her mother?

(A) 3

(B) 5

(C) 2

(D) 1

20. What would you expect to happen to the price of corn if there were a lack of rain and corn was scarce?

(A) The price of corn would increase.

(B) The price of corn would decrease.

(C) The price of corn would stay the same.

(D) There is not enough information.

GO ON

21. Julian buys a new pair of boots for $55. Which best describes what he does with the money?

Ⓐ saving

Ⓑ spending

Ⓒ income

Ⓓ giving

22. Bart has $124 in his savings account. After he makes an unplanned purchase, he has $105 left in his savings account. How much money did the unplanned purchase cost?

Ⓐ $19   Ⓒ $20

Ⓑ $229   Ⓓ $24

23. Alexis has $15. Tomorrow she will earn $12 at work. She wants to buy a new vest that costs $22. How much can Alexis spend today if she wants to buy the vest tomorrow?

Ⓐ $7   Ⓒ $10

Ⓑ $3   Ⓓ $5

24. Eric donates $15 to a hospital. Which best describes his donation?

Ⓐ income

Ⓑ spending

Ⓒ giving

Ⓓ saving

25. Casey has $45. She wants to buy four softballs for $12 each. Her father will lend her enough money to buy the softballs. How much will Casey need to borrow from her father on credit?

Record your answer and fill in the bubbles on the grid. Be sure to use the correct place value.

			.
⓪	⓪	⓪	
①	①	①	
②	②	②	
③	③	③	
④	④	④	
⑤	⑤	⑤	
⑥	⑥	⑥	
⑦	⑦	⑦	
⑧	⑧	⑧	
⑨	⑨	⑨	

GO ON

26. The size of a food crop can affect its price. When a crop is more plentiful, the cost will lower. The table shows the price for one pound of flour in different years.

Wheat Flour (price for one pound)	
Year	Price
2008	42¢
2009	52¢
2010	49¢
2011	48¢

In which year was the wheat crop probably the smallest?

(A) 2008   (C) 2010

(B) 2009   (D) 2011

27. Angelina borrows $5 from her friend to pay for a snack. Which best describes how she gets the money?

(A) income

(B) credit

(C) spending

(D) saving

28. Marta plans to save $20 each month to buy a bike. How much money will she have saved after 8 months?

(A) $28   (C) $140

(B) $160   (D) $80

29. Leo puts $10 aside each week for his education expenses. Which best describes what he does with his money?

(A) income   (C) giving

(B) credit   (D) saving

30. Henry plans to save $4 a week for a new bean bag chair. The chair costs $35, and he has $19 saved. Which of the following will result in Henry NOT being able to buy the chair?

(A) He continues to save and makes no unplanned purchases for 4 weeks.

(B) He saves for 2 more weeks and then buys a game.

(C) He spends $2 and then saves $5 a week for 4 weeks.

(D) He saves for 2 more weeks and then increases his savings to $8 a week for 2 weeks.

STOP

Prerequisite Skills Inventory Test

Item	Grade 2 Lesson	Grade 2 TEKS*	Common Error	Intervene with RtI* Tier 1 Lessons	Soar to Success Math
1	1.1	2.2.B	May not understand that a number can be written in different ways	8	2.17
2	3.4	2.2.C	May not know how to use comparative language	14	7.24
3	3.4	2.2.C	May not know how to use comparative language	14	7.24
4	2.4	2.2.E	May not understand how to locate the position of a number on a number line	15	15.13
5	2.2	2.2.D	May not know how to use the $<$, $>$, and $=$ symbols	11	7.26
6	3.5	2.2.D	May not know how to use the $<$, $>$, and $=$ symbols	11	7.26
7	4.3	2.3.A	May not understand that the more fractional parts, the smaller the parts are	19	5.04
8	4.1	2.3.A	May not be able to identify halves of a whole	17	5.04
9	4.5	2.3.C	May not understand how to identify fractional parts beyond one whole using words	21	5.07
10	6.3	2.4.B	May not understand how to break apart addends to add tens then add ones	29	10.30
11	4.4	2.3.D	May not be able to identify examples and non-examples of halves, fourths, and eighths	20	5.07
12	5.1	2.4.A	May not understand how to use doubles facts to add	22	10.14
13	5.4	2.4.A	May not understand how to use tens facts to subtract	25	10.29
14	7.4	2.4.B	May not add the third addend	33	10.37
15	8.1	2.4.B	May not regroup 10 ones as 1 ten	33	11.19
16	8.3	2.4.B	May add instead of subtracting	35	11.24
17	9.3	2.4.C	May not understand how to write a number sentence to represent the problem	37	11.26
18	10.7	2.4.C	May omit a step needed to solve the problem	42	11.17
19	10.8	2.4.D	May not understand how to write a number sentence to represent the problem	50	11.17
20	10.8	2.4.D	May not understand how to write a number sentence to represent the problem	52	11.17

*TEKS—Texas Essential Knowledge and Skills; **RtI**—Response to Intervention

Prerequisite Skills Inventory Test

Item	Grade 2 Lesson	Grade 2 TEKS*	Common Error	Intervene with RtI* Tier 1 Lessons	Soar to Success Math
21	11.1	2.5.A	May not include the value of a nickel	53	3.10, 3.11
22	11.2	2.5.B	May not understand how to use the dollar sign and the decimal point to show the value of a dollar	54	3.13
23	12.2	2.6.A	May not understand how to interpret multiplication situations	58	12.19
24	12.6	2.6.B	May not understand how to interpret division situations	62	13.08
25	13.1	2.7.A	May not know how to correctly identify an even or odd number	63	27.11
26	13.3	2.7.B	May not understand the meaning of 100 fewer	64	28.14
27	13.4	2.7.C	May not understand how to write a number sentence to represent a problem	66	70.02
28	13.5	2.7.C	May not understand how to write a number sentence to represent a problem	67	14.18
29	14.4	2.8.A	May miscount the number of vertices a two-dimensional shape has	68	38.18
30	15.2	2.8.B	May not be able to sort three-dimensional solids based on attributes	4	39.33
31	14.6	2.8.C	May not understand how to sort two-dimensional shapes by number of vertices	73	38.11
32	16.2	2.9.D	May not line up the zero mark of the ruler with the edge of the object when measuring	83	41.10
33	17.4	2.9.F	May not understand how to use square units to find the area of a rectangle	85	48.15
34	16.4	2.9.E	May have difficulty estimating the length of an object	84	41.10
35	18.1	2.9.G	May not read time correctly to the nearest minute	88	51.08, 51.10
36	19.5	2.10.C	May not understand how to use a pictograph	93	54.16
37	19.5	2.10.C	May not understand how to use a bar graph	93	54.16
38	19.7	2.10.D	May not know how to use a bar graph to make a prediction	96	54.15
39	20.3	2.11.C	May not understand that a deposit involves addition and a withdrawal involves subtraction	32	10.34
40	20.5	2.11.D	May not correctly calculate the amount of money to borrow for a given purchase	38	11.23, 11.24

*TEKS—Texas Essential Knowledge and Skills; **RtI**—Response to Intervention

Beginning-of-Year Test

Item	Lesson	TEKS*	Common Error	Intervene with RtI* Tier 1 Lessons	Soar to Success Math
1	11.1	3.4.J	May not understand related facts	3.40	30.36
2	16.2	3.6.C	May not count unit squares correctly	3.76	48.28
3	17.1	3.7.B	May find the area instead of perimeter	3.83	47.30
4	2.3	3.3.A	May have difficulty naming the shaded part	3.6	5.07, 5.09
5	20.1	3.9.A	May add instead of multiplying	3.39	12.49
6	1.2	3.2.A	May have difficulty decomposing numbers using base-ten blocks	3.2	2.25
7	11.3	3.4.I	May confuse odd and even	3.56	27.11
8	18.4	3.7.A	May not understand how to place fractions on a number line	3.82	35.15
9	9.3	3.4.G	May not understand how to use strategies to solve multiplication problems	3.43	12.23
10	18.2	3.7.C	May not add time intervals correctly	3.87	51.16
11	2.5	3.3.D	May not understand unit fractions	3.9	20.16
12	20.5	3.9.E	May multiply incorrect numbers	3.71	33.15, 33.16
13	20.4	3.9.D	May not complete all parts of the problem	3.64	71.03
14	14.2	3.5.A	May add instead of subtracting	3.67	11.22
15	14.7	3.5.D	May choose an incorrect factor	3.70	12.33
16	12.1	3.4.K	May divide by an incorrect number	3.51	13.15

*TEKS—Texas Essential Knowledge and Skills; RtI—Response to Intervention

Student's Name _____   Date _____

Beginning-of-Year Test (continued)

Item	Lesson	TEKS*	Common Error	Intervene with RtI* Tier 1 Lessons	Soar to Success Math
17	4.6	3.4.C	May not understand the value of coins and bills	3.25	4.15
18	18.6	3.7.D	May not understand units of capacity	3.92	43.09, 43.10
19	16.1	3.6.D	May not correctly decompose the figure	3.79	48.31
20	4.3	3.4.A	May not understand how to use properties to add three numbers	3.16	10.42
21	6.2	3.4.E	May add instead of multiplying	3.28	35.11
22	6.4	3.4.D	May not understand how to write multiplication sentences	3.26	12.35
23	18.7	3.7.E	May not know how many ounces are in one pound	3.90	42.05, 32.06
24	16.4	3.6.E	May not understand that equal parts can be different shapes	3.81	5.10
25	14.7	3.5.D	May divide instead of multiplying	3.70	12.33
26	2.2	3.3.C	May confuse numerator and denominator	3.8	5.08, 5.10
27	10.4	3.4.H	May have difficulty with multi-step problems	3.48	13.10
28	1.3	3.2.B	May have difficulty describing the place value of digits of multi-digit numbers	3.3	2.26
29	14.6	3.5.E	May not complete the pattern correctly.	3.71	33.15, 33.16
30	3.1	3.3.H	May not understand how to compare fractions that have the same denominator	3.13	9.30
31	3.5	3.3.F	May have difficulty identifying equivalent fractions using a model	3.12	9.32
32	14.4	3.5.B	May not divide into equal groups	3.68	30.35
33	1.5	3.2.D	May have difficulty ordering numbers	3.5	7.32, 7.33

*TEKS—Texas Essential Knowledge and Skills; **RtI**—Response to Intervention

Beginning-of-Year Test (continued)

Item	Lesson	TEKS*	Common Error	Intervene with RtI* Tier 1 Lessons	Soar to Success Math
34	3.4	3.3.G	May have difficulty identifying equivalent fractions on a number line	3.11	9.32
35	5.1	3.4.B	May not correctly round to the nearest hundred before estimating the difference	3.24	17.21
36	2.1	3.3.E	May not divide into equal parts	3.10	5.03
37	5.4	3.4.A	May add instead of subtracting	3.21	70.02
38	14.5	3.5.C	May not understand how to write an expression	3.69	12.43
39	8.5	3.4.F	May add instead of multiplying	3.38	12.30
40	15.5	3.6.A	May not correctly identify the shape	3.74	39.28, 39.29, 39.30, 39.33
41	1.4	3.2.C	May have difficulty identifying two consecutive multiples of 1,000 that a point on a number line is between	3.4	35.17
42	1.5	3.2.D	May have difficulty using symbols to compare whole numbers	3.5	7.32, 7.33
43	20.6	3.9.F	May not understand financial decisions involving spending.	3.21	70.02
44	15.1	3.6.B	May not understand that a rhombus and rectangle are parallelograms	3.72	38.31
45	8.1	3.4.K	May not complete both parts of the problem	3.60	12.31
46	2.4	3.3.B	May identify the fraction incorrectly	3.7	35.15
47	20.3	3.9.C	May not complete the steps of the entire problem	3.61	61.02
48	20.2	3.9.B	May not understand how availability and scarcity relate to cost	3.5	7.32, 7.33
49	19.2	3.8.B	May not understand how to use the key	3.94	54.12, 54.14
50	19.2	3.8.A	May not count correctly	3.94	54.12, 54.14

*TEKS—Texas Essential Knowledge and Skills; **RtI**—Response to Intervention

Student's Name _____ Date _____

Middle of Year Test

Item	Lesson	TEKS*	Common Error	Intervene with RtI* Tier 1 Lessons	Soar to Success Math
1	11.1	3.4.J	May not understand related facts	3.40	30.36
2	16.2	3.6.C	May not understand to use multiplication to find area	3.76	48.28
3	17.1	3.7.B	May find the area instead of perimeter	3.83	47.30
4	2.3	3.3.A	May have difficulty naming the shaded fractional part.	3.6	5.07, 5.09
5	20.1	3.9.A	May add instead of multiplying	3.39	12.49
6	1.2	3.2.A	May have difficulty decomposing numbers in standard form	3.2	2.25
7	11.3	3.4.I	May confuse odd and even	3.56	27.11
8	18.4	3.7.A	May not understand how to place fractions on a number line	3.82	35.15
9	9.3	3.4.G	May not understand how to use strategies to solve multiplication problems	3.43	12.23
10	18.2	3.7.C	May not subtract time intervals correctly	3.87	51.16
11	2.5	3.3.D	May not understand unit fractions	3.9	20.16
12	20.5	3.9.E	May not understand savings plans	3.71	33.15, 33.16
13	20.4	3.9.D	May not complete all parts of the problem	3.64	71.03
14	14.1	3.5.A	May subtract instead of adding	3.66	10.29, 10.30
15	14.7	3.5.D	May choose an incorrect factor	3.70	12.33
16	11.2	3.4.K	May add instead of multiply	3.50	13.21

*TEKS—Texas Essential Knowledge and Skills; **RtI**—Response to Intervention

Middle of Year Test (continued)

Item	Lesson	TEKS*	Common Error	Intervene with RtI* Tier 1 Lessons	Soar to Success Math
17	4.6	3.4.C	May not understand the value of bills	3.25	4.15
18	18.7	3.7.D	May not understand units of weight	3.90	42.05, 42.06
19	16.1	3.6.D	May not decompose the figure correctly	3.79	48.31
20	5.2	3.4.A	May not complete both parts of the problem	3.19	11.29, 11.30, 11.31, 11.32
21	6.1	3.4.E	May not understand repeated addition	3.27	12.27
22	6.4	3.4.D	May not understand arrays	3.26	12.35
23	18.8	3.7.E	May not understand tools for measuring mass	3.91	42.07, 42.08
24	16.4	3.6.E	May not understand how to represent parts with fractions	3.81	5.10
25	14.7	3.5.D	May multiply instead of dividing	3.70	12.33
26	2.2	3.3.C	May confuse numerator and denominator	3.8	5.08, 5.10
27	10.4	3.4.H	May not subtract before dividing	3.48	13.10
28	1.3	3.2.B	May have difficulty identifying the place value of digits of multi-digit numbers	3.3	2.26
29	14.6	3.5.E	May add instead of multiplying	3.71	33.15, 33.16
30	3.2	3.3.H	May not understand how to compare fractions that have the same numerator	3.14	9.29
31	3.5	3.3.F	May have difficulty identifying equivalent fractions using a number line	3.12	9.32
32	6.3	3.5.B	May add instead of multiplying	3.29	12.35, 12.37, 12.38
33	1.5	3.2.D	May have difficulty ordering numbers	3.5	7.32, 7.33

*TEKS—Texas Essential Knowledge and Skills; **RtI**—Response to Intervention

Student's Name _____ Date _____

Middle of Year Test (continued)

Item	Lesson	TEKS*	Common Error	Intervene with RtI* Tier 1 Lessons	Soar to Success Math
34	3.4	3.3.G	May have difficulty identifying equivalent fractions on a number line	3.11	9.32
35	4.2	3.4.B	May not correctly round	3.23	16.27
36	2.1	3.3.E	May not divide into equal parts	3.10	5.03
37	5.4	3.4.A	May subtract instead of adding	3.21	70.02
38	14.5	3.5.C	May have difficulty writing an expression	3.69	12.43
39	7.3	3.4.F	May not understand how division relates to multiplication	3.33	12.26, 12.28
40	15.5	3.6.A	May not correctly count vertices	3.74	39.28, 39.29, 39.30, 39.33
41	1.2	3.2.C	May have difficulty rounding to the nearest thousand	3.2	2.25
42	1.5	3.2.D	May have difficulty comparing numbers	3.5	7.32, 7.33
43	20.6	3.9.F	May not understand financial decisions	3.21	70.02
44	15.1	3.6.B	May not understand characteristics of a trapezoid	3.72	38.31
45	10.2	3.4.K	May not complete both parts of the problem	3.46	13.22
46	2.4	3.3.B	May identify the fraction incorrectly	3.7	35.15
47	20.3	3.9.C	May not complete both parts of the problem	3.61	61.02
48	20.2	3.9.B	May not understand how cost relates to availability and scarcity	3.5	7.32, 7.33
49	19.2	3.8.B	May not complete both parts of the problem	3.94	54.12, 54.14
50	19.2	3.8.A	May have difficulty reading the dot plot	3.94	54.12, 54.14

*TEKS—Texas Essential Knowledge and Skills; RtI—Response to Intervention

End of Year Test

Item	Lesson	TEKS*	Common Error	Intervene with RtI* Tier 1 Lessons	Soar to Success Math
1	11.1	3.4.J	May not understand related facts	3.40	30.36
2	16.2	3.6.C	May not count unit squares correctly	3.76	48.28
3	17.1	3.7.B	May find the area instead of perimeter	3.83	47.30
4	2.3	3.3.A	May have difficulty naming the shaded part	3.6	5.07, 5.09
5	20.1	3.9.A	May add instead of multiply	3.39	12.49
6	1.2	3.2.A	May have difficulty decomposing numbers using quick pictures	3.2	2.25
7	11.3	3.4.I	May confuse odd and even	3.56	27.11
8	18.4	3.7.A	May not understand how to place fractions on a number line	3.82	35.15
9	9.5	3.4.G	May not understand how to use mental math to multiply	3.39	12.49
10	18.3	3.7.C	May not understand intervals of time	3.88	51.16
11	2.5	3.3.D	May not understand unit fractions	3.9	20.16
12	20.5	3.9.E	May have used the extra information to solve the problem.	3.71	33.15, 33.16
13	20.4	3.9.D	May not complete all parts of the problem	3.64	71.03
14	14.1	3.5.A	May not complete all parts of the problem	3.66	10.29, 10.30
15	14.7	3.5.D	May add instead of multiply	3.70	12.33
16	12.1	3.4.K	May not complete all parts of the problem	3.51	13.15

*TEKS—Texas Essential Knowledge and Skills; **RtI**—Response to Intervention

End of Year Test (continued)

Item	Lesson	TEKS*	Common Error	Intervene with RtI* Tier 1 Lessons	Soar to Success Math
17	4.6	3.4.C	May not understand the value of coins	3.25	4.15
18	18.6	3.7.D	May not understand units of capacity	3.92	43.09, 43.10
19	16.1	3.6.D	May not correctly decompose the figure	3.79	48.31
20	4.3	3.4.A	May not complete all steps of the problem	3.16	10.42
21	6.2	3.4.E	May add instead of multiply	3.28	35.11
22	6.4	3.4.D	May not understand how to arrange an array of objects	3.26	12.35
23	18.7	3.7.E	May not know the number of cups in a pint	3.90	42.05, 42.06
24	16.4	3.6.E	May not understand how to divide figures	3.81	5.10
25	14.7	3.5.D	May add instead of multiply	3.70	12.33
26	2.2	3.3.C	May confuse numerator and denominator	3.8	5.08, 5.10
27	10.4	3.4.H	May not complete all parts of the problem	3.48	13.10
28	1.3	3.2.B	May have difficulty describing the place value of digits of multi-digit numbers	3.3	2.26
29	14.6	3.5.E	May not complete the pattern correctly	3.71	33.15, 33.16
30	3.1	3.3.H	May not understand how to compare fractions that have the same numerator	3.13	9.30
31	3.5	3.3.F	May have difficulty identifying equivalent fractions using a model	3.12	9.32
32	14.4	3.5.B	May not understand how to use the model to solve the problem	3.68	30.35
33	1.5	3.2.D	May have difficulty comparing numbers	3.5	7.32, 7.33

*TEKS—Texas Essential Knowledge and Skills; **RtI**—Response to Intervention

End of Year Test (continued)

Item	Lesson	TEKS*	Common Error	Intervene with RtI* Tier 1 Lessons	Soar to Success Math
34	3.4	3.3.G	May have difficulty identifying equivalent fractions on a number line	3.11	9.32
35	5.1	3.4.B	May round incorrectly	3.24	17.21
36	2.1	3.3.E	May not divide into equal parts	3.10	5.03
37	5.4	3.4.A	May not do both parts of the problem	3.21	70.02
38	14.5	3.5.C	May not understand how to write an expression	3.69	12.43
39	8.5	3.4.F	May add instead of multiply	3.38	12.30
40	15.5	3.6.A	May not correctly identify shape	3.74	39.28, 39.29, 39.30, 39.33
41	1.4	3.2.C	May have difficulty identifying two consecutive multiples of 1,000 that a point on a number line that is between	3.4	35.17
42	1.5	3.2.D	May have difficulty ordering numbers	3.5	7.32, 7.33
43	20.6	3.9.F	May not understand financial decisions	3.21	70.02
44	15.1	3.6.B	May not recognize the attributes of rectangles	3.72	38.31
45	8.1	3.4.K	May not complete all parts of the problem	3.60	12.31
46	2.4	3.3.B	May identify the fraction incorrectly	3.7	35.15
47	20.3	3.9.C	May not complete all steps of the problem	3.61	61.02
48	20.2	3.9.B	May not understand how availability and scarcity relate to cost	3.5	7.32, 7.33
49	19.2	3.8.B	May not read pictograph correctly	3.94	54.12, 54.14
50	19.2	3.8.A	May not understand the pictograph	3.94	54.12, 54.14

*TEKS—Texas Essential Knowledge and Skills; RtI—Response to Intervention

Student's Name _____ Date _____

Module 1 Test

Item	Lesson	TEKS*	Common Error	Intervene with RtI* Tier 1 Lessons	Soar to Success Math
1	1.2	2.A	May have difficulty composing numbers using base-ten blocks	3.2	2.25
2	1.2	2.A	May have difficulty decomposing numbers using base-ten blocks	3.2	2.25
3	1.3	2.A	May have difficulty decomposing numbers	3.3	2.26
4	1.3	2.B	May have difficulty describing the place value of digits of multi-digit numbers	3.3	2.26
5	1.4	2.C	May not know how to find the nearest hundred using a number line	3.4	35.17
6	1.5	2.D	May have difficulty ordering numbers	3.5	7.32, 7.33
7	1.5	2.D	May have difficulty using symbols to compare whole numbers	3.5	7.32, 7.33
8	1.3	2.B	May have difficulty describing the place value of digits of multi-digit numbers	3.3	2.26
9	1.5	2.A	May have difficulty decomposing numbers using quick pictures	3.5	7.32, 7.33
10	1.1	2.A	May have difficulty composing numbers	3.1	2.24
11	1.4	2.C	May have difficulty identifying a point on a number line that is between two consecutive multiples of 1,000	3.4	35.17
12	1.3	2.B	May have difficulty describing the place value of digits of multi-digit numbers	3.3	2.26
13	1.4	2.C	May not know how to find the nearest ten using a number line	3.4	35.17
14	1.4	2.C	May not know how to find the nearest ten thousand using a number line	3.4	35.17
15	1.2	2.C	May have difficulty rounding to the nearest thousand	3.2	2.25
16	1.1	2.A	May have difficulty composing numbers using quick pictures	3.1	2.24
17	1.2	2.A	May have difficulty decomposing numbers using expanded notation	3.2	2.25
18	1.5	2.D	May have difficulty ordering multi-digit numbers	3.5	7.32, 7.33
19	1.5	2.D	May have difficulty using symbols to compare whole numbers	3.5	7.32, 7.33
20	1.2	2.A	May have difficulty describing place value in multi-digit numbers	3.2	2.25

*TEKS—Texas Essential Knowledge and Skills; RtI—Response to Intervention

Student's Name _____ Date _____

Module 2 Test

Item	Lesson	TEKS*	Common Error	Intervene with RtI* Tier 1 Lessons	Soar to Success Math
1	2.3	3.A	May not understand how fractions relate to wholes	3.6	5.07, 5.09
2	2.4	3.A	May have difficulty understanding fraction models	3.7	35.15
3	2.4	3.B	May misunderstand placement of fractions on the number line	3.7	35.15
4	2.5	3.D	May not understand how to compose unit fractions to make a fraction	3.9	20.16
5	2.5	3.D	May not understand how to decompose a fraction as a sum of unit fractions	3.9	20.16
6	2.3	3.A	May have difficulty naming the shaded part	3.6	5.07, 5.09
7	2.1	3.E	May not divide into equal parts	3.10	5.03
8	2.3	3.A	May miscount shaded parts	3.6	5.07, 5.09
9	2.1	3.E	May not divide into equal parts	3.10	5.03
10	2.2	3.C	May confuse numerator and denominator	3.8	5.08, 5.10
11	2.4	3.A	May confuse the numerator and denominator	3.7	35.15
12	2.4	3.A	May miscount shaded parts	3.7	35.15
13	2.4	3.A	May misunderstand placement of fractions on the number line	3.7	35.15
14	2.4	3.A	May name the shaded part	3.7	35.15
15	2.1	3.E	May not understand how to divide the wholes	3.10	5.03
16	2.4	3.B	May have difficulty determining points on the number line	3.7	35.15
17	2.4	3.A	May confuse the denominator and the numerator	3.7	35.15
18	2.1	3.E	May not understand how to divide the wholes	3.10	5.03
19	2.3	3.A	May confuse the numerator and denominator	3.6	5.07, 5.09
20	2.4	3.B	May misunderstand placement of fractions on the number line	3.7	35.15

*TEKS—Texas Essential Knowledge and Skills; **RtI**—Response to Intervention

Student's Name _____   Date _____

Module 3 Test

Item	Lesson	TEKS*	Common Error	Intervene with RtI* Tier 1 Lessons	Soar to Success Math
1	3.4	3.G	May have difficulty identifying equivalent fractions on a number line	3.11	9.32
2	3.1	3.H	May not understand how to compare fractions that have the same denominator	3.13	9.30
3	3.1	3.A	May have difficulty representing fractions using fraction strips	3.13	9.30
4	3.2	3.H	May not understand how to compare fractions that have the same numerator	3.14	9.29
5	3.4	3.F	May have difficulty identifying equivalent fractions on a number line	3.11	9.32
6	3.1	3.H	May not understand how to compare fractions that have the same denominator	3.13	9.30
7	3.4	3.F	May have difficulty identifying equivalent fractions on a number line	3.11	9.32
8	3.2	3.H	May not understand how to compare fractions that have the same numerator	3.14	9.29
9	3.5	3.F	May have difficulty identifying equivalent fractions using a model	3.12	9.32
10	3.4	3.F	May have difficulty identifying equivalent fractions on a number line	3.11	9.32
11	3.4	3.F	May have difficulty identifying equivalent fractions using a model	3.11	9.32
12	3.4	3.A	May have difficulty representing fractions using models	3.11	9.32
13	3.4	3.B	May have difficulty identifying a fraction on a number line	3.11	9.32
14	3.1	3.H	May not understand how to compare fractions that have the same numerator	3.13	9.30
15	3.5	3.E	May not understand how to divide the whole into equal shares	3.12	9.32
16	3.1	3.H	May not understand how to compare fractions that have the same denominator	3.13	9.30
17	3.4	3.F	May have difficulty identifying equivalent fractions using a model	3.11	9.32
18	3.4	3.F	May have difficulty identifying equivalent fractions on a number line	3.11	9.32
19	3.2	3.H	May not understand how to compare fractions that have the same numerator	3.14	9.29
20	3.4	3.B	May have difficulty identifying equivalent fractions on a number line	3.11	9.32

*TEKS—Texas Essential Knowledge and Skills; **RtI**—Response to Intervention

Module 4 Test

Item	Lesson	TEKS*	Common Error	Intervene with RtI* Tier 1 Lessons	Soar to Success Math
1	4.2	4.B	May not correctly round to the nearest 100 before adding	3.27	16.27
2	4.6	4.C	May not know correct values of bills and coins	3.25	4.15
3	4.1	4.B	May round incorrectly	3.22	5.15, 5.17
4	4.4	4.A	May not regroup correctly	3.17	10.30
5	4.1	4.B	May not correctly round to the nearest 10 before adding	3.22	5.15, 5.17
6	4.3	4.A	May not know how to use properties to add three numbers	3.16	10.42
7	4.4	4.A	May not regroup correctly	3.17	10.30
8	4.3	4.A	May not know how to use the Commutative Property to add three numbers	3.16	10.42
9	4.2	4.B	May not correctly round to the nearest 10 before adding	3.27	16.27
10	4.3	4.A	May not know how to use properties to add three numbers	3.16	10.42
11	4.4	4.B	May not understand how to use compatible numbers to estimate sums	3.17	10.30
12	4.5	4.B	May have difficulty estimating sums of multi-step problems	3.18	10.41
13	4.4	4.A	May have difficulty solving multi-step addition problems	3.17	10.30
14	4.2	4.A	May round incorrectly	3.27	16.27
15	4.5	4.A	May have difficulty solving multi-step addition problems	3.18	10.41
16	4.6	4.C	May not know correct values of coins	3.25	4.15
17	4.1	4.B	May round up instead of down	3.22	5.15, 5.17
18	4.5	4.A	May not regroup	3.18	10.41
19	4.2	4.A	May not regroup	3.27	16.27
20	4.5	4.A	May not regroup	3.18	10.41

*TEKS—Texas Essential Knowledge and Skills; **RtI**—Response to Intervention

Student's Name _____ Date _____

Module 5 Test

Item	Lesson	TEKS*	Common Error	Intervene with RtI* Tier 1 Lessons	Soar to Success Math
1	5.2	4.A	May add instead of subtract	3.19	11.29, 11.30, 11.31, 11.32
2	5.2	4.A	May have difficulty using a strip diagram to model addition	3.19	11.29, 11.30, 11.31, 11.32
3	5.3	4.A	May have difficulty solving multi-step problems	3.20	11.29, 11.30, 11.31, 11.32
4	5.1	4.B	May not correctly round to the nearest ten before estimating the difference	3.24	17.21
5	5.1	4.B	May not correctly round to the nearest hundred before estimating the difference	3.24	17.21
6	5.4	4.A	May have difficulty solving multi-step problems	3.21	70.02
7	5.2	4.A	May add instead of subtracting	3.19	11.29, 11.30, 11.31, 11.32
8	5.2	4.A	May not regroup	3.19	11.29, 11.30, 11.31, 11.32
9	5.1	4.B	May not understand how to use compatible numbers to estimate	3.24	17.21
10	5.3	4.A	May have difficulty solving multi-step problems	3.20	11.29, 11.30, 11.31, 11.32
11	5.2	4.A	May add instead of subtract	3.19	11.29, 11.30, 11.31, 11.32
12	5.4	4.A	May not complete both steps of the problem	3.21	70.02
13	5.1	4.B	May not correctly round to the nearest hundred before estimating the difference	3.24	17.21
14	5.3	4.A	May have difficulty solving multi-step problems	3.20	11.29, 11.30, 11.31, 11.32
15	5.3	4.A	May not regroup	3.20	11.29, 11.30, 11.31, 11.32
16	5.4	4.A	May add instead of subtract	3.21	70.02
17	5.1	4.B	May not correctly round to the nearest ten before estimating the difference	3.24	17.21
18	5.2	4.A	May have difficulty solving multi-step problems	3.19	11.29, 11.30, 11.31, 11.32
19	5.1	4.B	May not correctly round to the nearest hundred before estimating the difference	3.24	17.21
20	5.3	4.A	May not regroup	3.20	11.29, 11.30, 11.31, 11.32

*TEKS—Texas Essential Knowledge and Skills; RtI—Response to Intervention

Student's Name _____ Date _____

Unit 1 Test

Item	Lesson	TEKS*	Common Error	Intervene with RtI* Tier 1 Lessons	Soar to Success Math
1	2.5	3.D	May not understand unit fractions	3.9	20.16
2	4.6	4.C	May not understand the value of coins	3.25	4.15
3	5.4	4.A	May subtract instead of add	3.21	70.02
4	1.5	2.D	May have difficulty ordering numbers	3.5	7.32, 7.33
5	3.2	3.H	May not understand how to compare fractions that have the same numerator	3.14	9.29
6	2.1	3.E	May not divide into equal parts	3.10	5.03
7	4.2	4.B	May not understand how to use compatible numbers to estimate sums	3.23	16.27
8	1.3	2.B	May have difficulty describing the place value of digits of multi-digit numbers	3.3	2.26
9	4.5	4.A	May not regroup correctly	3.18	10.41
10	3.4	3.F	May have difficulty identifying equivalent fractions using a number line	3.11	9.32
11	5.1	4.B	May not round to the nearest ten	3.24	17.21
12	2.3	3.A	May identify the fraction incorrectly	3.6	5.07, 5.09
13	4.4	4.A	May have difficulty solving multi-step addition problems	3.17	10.30
14	1.1	2.A	May have difficulty decomposing numbers	3.1	2.24
15	4.3	4.A	May not understand how to use properties to add three numbers	3.16	10.42
16	2.3	3.A	May have difficulty naming the shaded part	3.6	5.07, 5.09
17	1.4	2.C	May have difficulty identifying which multiples of 1,000 a point is between on a number line	3.4	35.17
18	2.2	3.C	May confuse numerator and denominator	3.8	5.08, 5.10
19	4.2	4.B	May not correctly round to the nearest 10 before adding	3.23	16.27
20	3.1	3.H	May not understand how to compare fractions that have the same denominator	3.13	9.30

*TEKS—Texas Essential Knowledge and Skills; **RtI**—Response to Intervention

Unit 1 Test (continued)

Item	Lesson	TEKS*	Common Error	Intervene with RtI* Tier 1 Lessons	Soar to Success Math
21	5.1	4.B	May round incorrectly	3.24	17.21
22	1.2	2.A	May have difficulty decomposing numbers using base-ten blocks	3.2	2.25
23	2.4	3.A	May not understand placement of fractions on the number line	3.7	35.15
24	3.4	3.G	May have difficulty identifying equivalent fractions on a number line	3.11	9.32
25	5.4	4.A	May add instead of subtract	3.21	70.02
26	3.5	3.F	May have difficulty identifying equivalent fractions using a model	3.12	9.32
27	4.5	4.B	May have difficulty estimating sums of multi-step problems	3.18	10.41
28	3.1	3.H	May not understand how to compare fractions that have the same denominator	3.13	9.30
29	1.5	2.D	May have difficulty using symbols to compare whole numbers	3.5	7.32, 7.33
30	1.2	2.A	May have difficulty composing numbers using base-ten blocks	3.2	2.25

*TEKS—Texas Essential Knowledge and Skills; RtI—Response to Intervention

Module 6 Test

Item	Lesson	TEKS*	Common Error	Intervene with RtI* Tier 1 Lessons	Soar to Success Math
1	6.4	4.K	May add instead of multiply	3.26	12.35
2	6.3	4.K	May have difficulty solving multi-step problems	3.29	12.35, 12.37, 12.38
3	6.1	4.E	May not understand how groups of objects relate to multiplication	3.27	12.27
4	6.2	4.K	May add instead of multiply	3.28	35.11
5	6.5	4.E	May not understand arrays	3.30	12.32
6	6.6	4.K	May add instead of multiply	3.59	12.24
7	6.1	4.E	May not understand how multiplication is related to addition	3.27	12.27
8	6.5	4.K	May not understand how to use the Commutative Property of Multiplication	3.30	12.32
9	6.2	4.E	May add instead of multiply	3.28	35.11
10	6.3	4.K	May have difficulty solving multi-step problems	3.29	12.35, 12.37, 12.38
11	6.2	4.E	May not skip count correctly	3.28	35.11
12	6.3	4.K	May add instead of multiply	3.29	12.35, 12.37, 12.38
13	6.5	4.E	May not understand how to use the Commutative Property of Multiplication	3.30	12.32
14	6.5	4.K	May have difficulty solving multi-step problems	3.30	12.32
15	6.4	4.D	May not understand arrays	3.26	12.35
16	6.1	4.D	May not understand how addition is related to multiplication	3.27	12.27
17	6.6	4.K	May subtract instead of multiply	3.59	12.24
18	6.5	4.K	May not understand arrays	3.30	12.32
19	6.6	4.K	May add or subtract instead of multiply	3.59	12.24
20	6.4	4.D	May miscount the number of squares in each row of the array	3.26	12.35

TEKS—Texas Essential Knowledge and Skills; **RtI**—Response to Intervention

Student's Name _____ Date _____

Module 7 Test

Item	Lesson	TEKS*	Common Error	Intervene with RtI* Tier 1 Lessons	Soar to Success Math
1	7.4	4.K	May not understand the array	3.34	12.22, 12.23
2	7.1	4.K	May add instead of multiply	3.31	12.21, 12.25
3	7.3	4.E	May add instead of multiply	3.33	12.26, 12.28
4	7.2	4.E	May multiply incorrectly	3.32	12.22, 12.23
5	7.4	4.K	May not understand the Distributive Property	3.34	12.22, 12.23
6	7.2	4.E	May add instead of multiply	3.32	12.22, 12.23
7	7.4	4.E	May miscount the number of rows or circles in each row	3.34	12.22, 12.23
8	7.3	4.K	May have difficulty solving multi-step problems	3.33	12.26, 12.28
9	7.4	4.K	May add instead of multiply	3.34	12.22, 12.23
10	7.3	4.K	May have difficulty solving multi-step problems	3.33	12.26, 12.28
11	7.4	4.K	May not understand the array	3.34	12.22, 12.23
12	7.1	4.K	May not multiply correctly	3.31	12.21, 12.25
13	7.1	4.E	May not understand how to use doubles to solve the problem	3.31	12.21, 12.25
14	7.2	4.E	May skip count incorrectly	3.32	12.22, 12.23
15	7.4	4.K	May have difficulty solving multi-step problems	3.34	12.22, 12.23
16	7.3	4.K	May add instead of multiply	3.33	12.26, 12.28
17	7.4	4.K	May not understand the array	3.34	12.22, 12.23
18	7.3	4.K	May multiply incorrectly	3.33	12.26, 12.28
19	7.1	4.E	May not understand how equal groups relate to multiplication	3.31	12.21, 12.25
20	7.3	4.K	May have difficulty solving multi-step problems	3.33	12.26, 12.28

*TEKS—Texas Essential Knowledge and Skills; **RtI**—Response to Intervention

© Houghton Mifflin Harcourt Publishing Company

Module 8 Test

Item	Lesson	TEKS*	Common Error	Intervene with RtI* Tier 1 Lessons	Soar to Success Math
1	8.4	4.E	May miscount jumps on the number line	3.36	12.29
2	8.2	4.F	May not recall multiplication facts correctly	3.37	12.50
3	8.1	4.K	May have difficulty solving multi-step problems	3.60	12.31
4	8.5	4.K	May multiply incorrectly	3.38	12.30
5	8.3	4.E	May not understand how addition relates to multiplication	3.35	12.38
6	8.4	4.K	May not recall multiplication facts correctly	3.36	12.29
7	8.1	4.E	May not understand how arrays relate to multiplication	3.60	12.31
8	8.5	4.F	May not recall multiplication facts correctly	3.38	12.30
9	8.6	4.K	May have difficulty solving multi-step problems	3.61	61.02
10	8.5	4.K	May not recall multiplication facts correctly	3.38	12.30
11	8.1	4.K	May not understand the array	3.60	12.31
12	8.4	4.K	May not recall multiplication facts correctly	3.36	12.29
13	8.6	4.K	May have difficulty solving multi-step problems	3.61	61.02
14	8.1	4.K	May not understand the array	3.60	12.31
15	8.3	4.E	May not understand how addition relates to multiplication	3.35	12.38
16	8.4	4.E	May not skip count correctly	3.36	12.29
17	8.1	4.K	May have difficulty solving multi-step problems	3.60	12.31
18	8.5	4.F	May add instead of multiply	3.38	12.30
19	8.2	4.K	May not understand how to use the Distributive Property to solve the problem	3.37	12.50
20	8.3	4.E	May confuse the terms odd and even	3.35	12.38

*TEKS—Texas Essential Knowledge and Skills; RtI—Response to Intervention

Student's Name _____ Date _____

Module 9 Test

Item	Lesson	TEKS*	Common Error	Intervene with RtI* Tier 1 Lessons	Soar to Success Math
1	9.4	3.4.E	May not add partial products	3.44	12.46
2	9.3	3.4.G	May not understand how to use the Commutative Property to multiply	3.43	12.23
3	9.1	3.4.G	May not understand how to multiply multiples of 10	3.41	12.51
4	9.5	3.4.G	May not add the regrouped ten	3.39	12.49
5	9.2	3.4.G	May not know products of multiplication facts	3.42	12.23, 12.41
6	9.3	3.4.G	May not understand the Associative Property	3.43	12.23
7	9.1	3.4.K	May not understand how to multiply multiples of 10	3.41	12.51
8	9.5	3.4.G	May not regroup correctly	3.39	12.49
9	9.4	3.4.G	May not add partial products	3.44	12.46
10	9.1	3.4.K	May not complete both steps of the problem	3.41	12.51
11	9.3	3.4.G	May not know products of multiplication facts	3.43	12.23
12	9.1	3.4.E	May not understand how the model relates to multiplication	3.41	12.51
13	9.4	3.4.K	May not complete both steps of the problem	3.44	12.46
14	9.3	3.4.G	May not know products of multiplication facts	3.43	12.23
15	9.2	3.4.G	May not know products of multiplication facts	3.42	12.23, 12.41
16	9.4	3.4.K	May not add partial products	3.44	12.46
17	9.1	3.4.G	May not know products of multiplication facts	3.41	12.51
18	9.5	3.4.G	May not regroup	3.39	12.49
19	9.4	3.4.K	May not complete both steps of the problem	3.44	12.46
20	9.1	3.4.G	May not understand how to use the Distributive Property to multiply	3.41	12.51

*TEKS—Texas Essential Knowledge and Skills; **RtI**—Response to Intervention

Module 10 Test

Item	Lesson	TEKS*	Common Error	Intervene with RtI* Tier 1 Lessons	Soar to Success Math
1	10.2	3.4.K	May not divide into equal groups	3.46	13.22
2	10.1	3.4.H	May not divide into equal groups	3.45	13.23
3	10.4	3.4.K	May not complete both parts of the problem	3.48	3.10
4	10.5	3.4.K	May not understand how to use strategies to solve division problems	3.49	13.17
5	10.3	3.4.K	May not understand how to use strategies to solve division problems	3.47	13.23
6	10.1	3.4.K	May not add before dividing	3.45	13.23
7	10.2	3.4.K	May subtract instead of dividing	3.46	13.22
8	10.3	3.4.K	May not complete both parts of the problem	3.47	13.23
9	10.5	3.4.H	May subtract instead of dividing	3.49	13.17
10	10.5	3.4.K	May not add before dividing	3.49	13.17
11	10.4	3.4.K	May not understand how to use strategies to solve division problems	3.48	3.10
12	10.2	3.4.H	May not understand how to use strategies to solve division problems	3.46	13.22
13	10.3	3.4.H	May not understand how to use strategies to solve division problems	3.47	13.23
14	10.5	3.4.K	May not complete both parts of the problem	3.49	13.17
15	10.1	3.4.K	May not understand how to use strategies to solve division problems	3.45	13.23
16	10.1	3.4.K	May not understand how to use strategies to solve division problems	3.45	13.23
17	10.2	3.4.K	May not complete both parts of the problem	3.46	13.22
18	10.4	3.4.H	May not complete both parts of the problem	3.48	3.10
19	10.5	3.4.K	May not understand how to use strategies to solve division problems	3.49	13.17
20	10.3	3.4.H	May not understand how to use strategies to solve division problems	3.47	13.23

*TEKS—Texas Essential Knowledge and Skills; **RtI**—Response to Intervention

Student's Name _____ Date _____

Module 11 Test

Item	Lesson	TEKS*	Common Error	Intervene with RtI* Tier 1 Lessons	Soar to Success Math
1	11.2	3.4.H	May subtract instead of dividing	3.50	13.21
2	11.3	3.4.I	May confuse even and odd numbers	3.56	27.11
3	11.1	3.4.F	May not understand related facts	3.40	30.36
4	11.3	3.4.I	May confuse even and odd numbers	3.56	27.11
5	11.2	3.4.H	May not understand how to divide by 1	3.50	13.21
6	11.1	3.4.J	May not understand related facts	3.40	30.36
7	11.2	3.4.K	May not understand how to divide with 0	3.50	13.21
8	11.3	3.4.I	May confuse even and odd numbers	3.56	27.11
9	11.2	3.4.K	May not understand how to divide by 1	3.50	13.21
10	11.3	3.4.I	May confuse even and odd numbers	3.56	27.11
11	11.1	3.4.F	May not understand related facts	3.40	30.36
12	11.2	3.4.H	May not understand how to divide by 0	3.50	13.21
13	11.3	3.4.I	May confuse even and odd numbers	3.56	27.11
14	11.2	3.4.H	May not correctly recall multiplication facts	3.50	13.21
15	11.1	3.4.J	May not understand related facts	3.40	30.36
16	11.1	3.4.F	May not understand related facts	3.40	30.36
17	11.3	3.4.I	May confuse odd and even	3.56	27.11
18	11.2	3.4.K	May not understand how to divide by 1	3.50	13.21
19	11.3	3.4.I	May confuse odd and even	3.56	27.11
20	11.1	3.4.J	May not understand related facts	3.40	30.36

*TEKS—Texas Essential Knowledge and Skills; **RtI**—Response to Intervention

Student's Name _____ Date _____

Module 12 Test

Item	Lesson	TEKS*	Common Error	Intervene with RtI* Tier 1 Lessons	Soar to Success Math
1	12.2	3.4.K	May not add before dividing	3.62	13.12, 13.18
2	12.1	3.4.K	May subtract instead of dividing	3.51	13.15
3	12.5	3.4.F	May not recall the correct multiplication fact to help divide	3.53	13.13, 13.20, 13.23
4	12.3	3.4.K	May not understand how to use a number line to model division	3.63	13.12, 13.16
5	12.4	3.4.K	May subtract instead of dividing	3.52	13.13, 13.19
6	12.3	3.4.K	May not complete all steps of the multi-step problem	3.63	13.12, 13.16
7	12.1	3.4.H	May not divide into equal groups	3.51	13.15
8	12.2	3.4.J	May not understand the relationship between multiplication and division	3.62	13.12, 13.18
9	12.5	3.4.K	May not complete all steps of the multi-step problem	3.53	13.13, 13.20, 13.23
10	12.4	3.4.K	May not complete all steps of the multi-step problem	3.52	13.13, 13.19
11	12.1	3.4.H	May subtract instead of dividing	3.51	13.15
12	12.2	3.4.K	May not understand how to relate an array model to division	3.62	13.12, 13.18
13	12.1	3.4.K	May subtract and not divide or divide and not subtract	3.51	13.15
14	12.5	3.4.F	May subtract instead of dividing	3.53	13.13, 13.20, 13.23
15	12.3	3.4.K	May recall facts incorrectly	3.63	13.12, 13.16
16	12.4	3.4.K	May not recall the correct division fact	3.52	13.13, 13.19
17	12.3	3.4.K	May not complete all steps of the multi-step problem	3.63	13.12, 13.16
18	12.1	3.4.H	May recall facts incorrectly	3.51	13.15
19	12.2	3.4.J	May not complete all steps of the multi-step problem	3.62	13.12, 13.18
20	12.5	3.4.K	May divide incorrectly	3.53	13.13, 13.20, 13.23

*TEKS—Texas Essential Knowledge and Skills; **RtI**—Response to Intervention

© Houghton Mifflin Harcourt Publishing Company

Child's Name _____   Date _____

Module 13 Test

Item	Lesson	TEKS*	Common Error	Intervene with RtI* Tier 1 Lessons	Soar to Success Math
1	13.1	3.4.H	May not divide into equal groups	3.54	13.14, 13.22, 13.23
2	13.4	3.4.J	May subtract or add instead of dividing	3.55	13.14, 13.22, 13.23
3	13.3	3.4.K	May not understand how the model relates to division	3.58	13.14, 13.22, 13.23
4	13.2	3.4.K	May subtract instead of divide	3.57	13.14, 13.22, 13.23
5	13.3	3.4.H	May not divide into equal groups	3.58	13.14, 13.22, 13.23
6	13.1	3.4.K	May not understand how the model relates to division	3.54	13.14, 13.22, 13.23
7	13.5	3.4.K	May have difficulty dividing in multi-step problems	3.64	71.13
8	13.4	3.4.K	May not correctly recall division facts	3.55	13.14, 13.22, 13.23
9	13.2	3.4.K	May subtract instead of divide	3.57	13.14, 13.22, 13.23
10	13.1	3.4.J	May not understand the relationship between multiplication and division	3.54	13.14, 13.22, 13.23
11	13.3	3.4.K	May not understand how the model relates to division	3.58	13.14, 13.22, 13.23
12	13.2	3.4.K	May have difficulty dividing in multi-step problems	3.57	13.14, 13.22, 13.23
13	13.4	3.4.H	May not divide into equal groups	3.55	13.14, 13.22, 13.23
14	13.5	3.4.K	May have difficulty dividing in multi-step problems	3.64	71.13
15	13.1	3.4.K	May not understand how the model relates to division	3.54	13.14, 13.22, 13.23
16	13.3	3.4.K	May not understand how the model relates to division	3.58	13.14, 13.22, 13.23
17	13.2	3.4.J	May not understand how multiplication relates to division	3.57	13.14, 13.22, 13.23
18	13.3	3.4.K	May not divide into equal groups	3.58	13.14, 13.22, 13.23
19	13.4	3.4.H	May not divide into equal groups	3.55	13.14, 13.22, 13.23
20	13.3	3.4.K	May not understand how the model relates to division	3.58	13.14, 13.22, 13.23

*TEKS—Texas Essential Knowledge and Skills; **RtI**—Response to Intervention

Student's Name _____ Date _____

Unit 2 Test

Item	Lesson	TEKS*	Common Error	Intervene with RtI* Tier 1 Lessons	Soar to Success Math
1	7.3	3.4.K	May not complete both steps of the problem	3.33	12.26, 12.28
2	8.5	3.4.F	May not recall multiplication facts correctly	3.38	12.30
3	12.1	3.4.H	May not divide into equal groups	3.51	13.15
4	10.5	3.4.K	May not understand how to use strategies to solve division problems	3.49	13.17
5	6.2	3.4.E	May add instead of multiply	3.28	35.11
6	11.3	3.4.I	May confuse odd and even	3.56	27.11
7	12.2	3.4.J	May not understand the relationship between multiplication and division	3.62	13.12, 13.18
8	9.1	3.4.G	May not correctly recall multiplication fact	3.41	12.51
9	7.1	3.4.E	May not understand how to use doubles to solve the problem	3.31	12.21, 12.25
10	8.6	3.4.K	May not complete both parts of the problem	3.61	61.02
11	12.5	3.4.K	May not understand how to relate model to division	3.53	13.13, 13.20, 13.23
12	6.5	3.4.E	May not correctly recall multiplication fact	3.30	12.32
13	9.4	3.4.E	May not understand how the model relates to multiplication	3.44	12.46
14	7.1	3.4.K	May add instead of multiply	3.31	12.21, 12.25
15	11.3	3.4.I	May confuse odd and even	3.56	27.11

*TEKS—Texas Essential Knowledge and Skills; **RtI**—Response to Intervention

Unit 2 Test (continued)

Item	Lesson	TEKS*	Common Error	Intervene with RtI* Tier 1 Lessons	Soar to Success Math
16	10.4	3.4.H	May not complete both parts of the problem	3.48	13.10
17	12.4	3.4.K	May not complete all steps of the multistep problem	3.52	13.13, 13.19
18	9.5	3.4.G	May not regroup correctly	3.39	12.49
19	6.3	3.4.K	May not complete both parts of the problem	3.29	12.35, 12.37, 12.38
20	7.4	3.4.K	May not complete both steps of the problem	3.34	12.22, 12.23
21	8.1	3.4.E	May not understand how arrays relate to multiplication	3.60	12.31
22	11.1	3.4.F	May not understand related facts	3.40	30.36
23	10.5	3.4.K	May not complete both parts of the problem	3.49	13.17
24	9.3	3.4.G	May only multiply 2 numbers	3.43	12.23
25	8.4	3.4.K	May not recall multiplication facts correctly	3.36	12.29
26	6.4	3.4.D	May miscount the number of squares in each row of the array	3.26	12.35
27	9.1	3.4.G	May not understand how to use Distributive Property to solve	3.41	12.51
28	12.2	3.4.K	May not add before dividing	3.62	13.12, 13.18
29	10.1	3.4.K	May not understand how to use strategies to solve division problems	3.45	13.23
30	6.4	3.4.D	May not understand arrays	3.26	12.35

*TEKS—Texas Essential Knowledge and Skills; **RtI**—Response to Intervention

Unit 3 Test

Item	Lesson	TEKS*	Common Error	Intervene with RtI* Tier 1 Lessons	Soar to Success Math
1	14.4	3.5.B	May not use the correct multiplication fact to help divide	3.68	30.35
2	14.2	3.5.A	May not complete both parts of the problem	3.67	11.2
3	14.7	3.5.D	May choose an incorrect factor	3.70	12.33
4	14.6	3.5.E	May not complete the pattern correctly	3.71	33.15, 33.16
5	14.5	3.5.C	May not understand how to write a comparison as multiplication	3.69	12.43
6	14.1	3.5.A	May not complete both parts of the problem	3.66	10.29, 10.30
7	14.4	3.5.B	May not relate multiplication to division	3.68	30.35
8	14.2	3.5.A	May add instead of subtracting	3.67	11.2
9	14.7	3.5.B	May find an incorrect factor	3.70	12.33
10	14.4	3.5.B	May not recall division fact correctly	3.68	30.35
11	14.3	3.5.B	May not complete all parts of the problem	3.65	27.12, 10.23
12	14.1	3.5.A	May miscount blocks	3.66	10.29, 10.30
13	14.7	3.5.D	May divide instead of multiplying	3.70	12.33
14	14.2	3.5.A	May not complete both parts of the problem	3.67	11.2
15	14.6	3.5.E	May not multiply correctly	3.71	33.15, 33.16

TEKS—Texas Essential Knowledge and Skills; **RtI**—Response to Intervention

Unit 3 Test (continued)

Item	Lesson	TEKS*	Common Error	Intervene with RtI* Tier 1 Lessons	Soar to Success Math
16	14.4	3.5.B	May not understand arrays	3.68	30.35
17	14.1	3.5.A	May add incorrectly	3.66	10.29, 10.30
18	14.4	3.5.B	May not complete both parts of the problem	3.68	30.35
19	14.7	3.5.D	May not understand how to find the missing number	3.70	12.33
20	14.4	3.5.B	May not complete both parts of the problem	3.68	30.35
21	14.3	3.5	May not determine the correct pattern	3.65	27.12, 10.23
22	14.7	3.5.D	May not relate division to multiplication	3.70	12.33
23	14.2	3.5.A	May not complete both parts of the problem	3.67	11.2
24	14.1	3.5.A	May not add correctly	3.66	10.29, 10.30
25	14.7	3.5.B	May not complete both parts of the problem	3.70	12.33
26	14.4	3.5.B	May miscount squares in the array	3.68	30.35
27	14.4	3.5.B	May multiply incorrectly	3.68	30.35
28	14.7	3.5.B	May not correctly recall division fact	3.70	12.33
29	14.1	3.5.A	May not complete both parts of the problem	3.66	10.29, 10.30
30	14.2	3.5.A	May add instead of subtracting	3.67	11.2

*TEKS—Texas Essential Knowledge and Skills; **RtI**—Response to Intervention

Student's Name _____ Date _____

Module 15 Test

Item	Lesson	TEKS*	Common Error	Intervene with RtI* Tier 1 Lessons	Soar to Success Math
1	15.3	3.6.B	May not understand characteristics of a quadrilateral	3.73	38.31
2	15.5	3.6.A	May not correctly count the faces	3.74	39.28, 39.29, 39.30, 39.33
3	15.1	3.6.B	May not understand that a square is also a rhombus	3.72	38.31
4	15.5	3.6.A	May not correctly name three-dimensional solids	3.74	39.28, 39.29, 39.30, 39.33
5	15.1	3.6.A	May not correctly name quadrilaterals	3.72	38.31
6	15.4	3.6.E	May not understand congruence	3.80	38.17, 40.17
7	15.1	3.6.B	May not understand how to classify quadrilaterals	3.72	38.31
8	15.2	3.6.B	May not correctly name quadrilaterals	3.75	38.31
9	15.5	3.6.A	May not correctly name three-dimensional solids	3.74	39.28, 39.29, 39.30, 39.33
10	15.2	3.6.B	May not correctly identify plane shapes	3.75	38.31
11	15.1	3.6.A	May not understand characteristics of a trapezoid	3.72	38.31
12	15.2	3.6.B	May not correctly identify parallelograms	3.75	38.31
13	15.5	3.6.A	May not correctly name three-dimensional solids	3.74	39.28, 39.29, 39.30, 39.33
14	15.4	3.6.E	May not understand congruence	3.80	38.17, 40.17
15	15.1	3.6.B	May not understand attributes of quadrilaterals	3.72	38.31
16	15.3	3.6.B	May not understand attributes of quadrilaterals	3.73	38.31
17	15.5	3.6.A	May not correctly name three-dimensional solids	3.74	39.28, 39.29, 39.30, 39.33
18	15.5	3.6.A	May not correctly name three-dimensional solids	3.74	39.28, 39.29, 39.30, 39.33
19	15.5	3.6.A	May not correctly name three-dimensional solids	3.74	39.28, 39.29, 39.30, 39.33
20	15.5	3.6.A	May not understand characteristics of a three-dimensional solid	3.74	39.28, 39.29, 39.30, 39.33

*TEKS—Texas Essential Knowledge and Skills; **RtI**—Response to Intervention

Module 16 Test

Item	Lesson	TEKS*	Common Error	Intervene with RtI* Tier 1 Lessons	Soar to Success Math
1	16.2	3.6.C	May not count unit squares correctly	3.76	48.28
2	16.5	3.6.D	May not understand how to complete a multi-step problem	3.78	48.26
3	16.4	3.6.E	May not understand unit fractions	3.81	5.10
4	16.1	3.6.D	May not understand how to complete a multi-step problem	3.79	48.31
5	16.3	3.6.C	May not understand how to find the area of a rectangle	3.76	48.28
6	16.4	3.6.E	May not understand unit fractions	3.81	5.10
7	16.4	3.6.E	May have difficulty decomposing figures	3.81	5.10
8	16.1	3.6.D	May not add areas of all of the rectangles	3.79	48.31
9	16.4	3.6.E	May not understand that equal parts can have different shapes	3.81	5.10
10	16.5	3.6.C	May not complete both parts of the problem	3.78	48.26
11	16.2	3.6.C	May miscount the number of rows and columns	3.76	48.28
12	16.4	3.6.E	May not understand that equal parts can have different shapes	3.81	5.10
13	16.1	3.6.D	May not correctly decompose the figure	3.79	48.31
14	16.4	3.6.E	May not understand unit fractions	3.81	5.10
15	16.3	3.6.C	May not understand how area changes relate to changes in length or width	3.76	48.28
16	16.5	3.6.D	May not decompose figure correctly	3.78	48.26

*TEKS—Texas Essential Knowledge and Skills; RtI—Response to Intervention

Student's Name _____ Date _____

Module 17 Test

Item	Lesson	TEKS*	Common Error	Intervene with RtI* Tier 1 Lessons	Soar to Success Math
1	17.1	3.7.B	May not add the lengths of all the sides	3.83	47.30
2	17.1	3.7.B	May not add the lengths of all the sides	3.83	47.30
3	17.2	3.7.B	May not add the lengths of all the sides	3.84	47.30
4	17.3	3.7.B	May not understand how to find the length of the unknown side	3.85	47.31
5	17.2	3.7.B	May add the lengths of only two sides	3.84	47.30
6	17.3	3.7.B	May not understand how to find the length of the unknown side	3.85	47.31
7	17.1	3.7.B	May miscount the units	3.83	47.30
8	17.2	3.7.B	May not add the measurements correctly	3.84	47.30
9	17.3	3.7.B	May not understand how to find the length of the unknown side	3.85	47.31
10	17.3	3.7.B	May not understand how to find the length of the unknown side	3.85	47.31
11	17.1	3.7.B	May not add the lengths of all the sides	3.83	47.30
12	17.2	3.7.B	May not know that a square has equal side lengths	3.84	47.30
13	17.3	3.7.B	May not understand how to find the length of the unknown side	3.85	47.31
14	17.1	3.7.B	May miscount the units	3.83	47.30
15	17.2	3.7.B	May not add the lengths of all the sides	3.84	47.30
16	17.3	3.7.B	May not understand how to find the length of the unknown side	3.85	47.31
17	17.1	3.7.B	May not add the lengths of all the sides	3.83	47.30
18	17.1	3.7.B	May miscount the units	3.83	47.30
19	17.2	3.7.B	May not add the measurements correctly	3.84	47.30

*TEKS—Texas Essential Knowledge and Skills; **RtI**—Response to Intervention

Student's Name _____ Date _____

Module 18 Test

Item	Lesson	TEKS*	Common Error	Intervene with RtI* Tier 1 Lessons	Soar to Success Math
1	18.3	3.7.C	May have difficulty solving problems that involve elapsed time	3.88	51.16
2	18.5	3.7.D, 3.7.E	May not understand how to convert units of capacity	3.89	43.07, 43.11
3	18.1	3.7.C	May not count minutes correctly	3.86	51.16
4	18.4	3.7.A	May not understand how to locate points on a number line	3.82	35.15
5	18.2	3.7.C	May have difficulty solving problems that involve elapsed time	3.87	51.16
6	18.6	3.7.D, 3.7.E	May not know appropriate units for liquid volume	3.92	43.9, 43.10
7	18.7	3.7.D, 3.7.E	May not understand customary units of weight	3.90	42.05, 42.06
8	18.1	3.7.C	May not count minutes correctly	3.86	51.16
9	18.3	3.7.C	May have difficulty solving multi-step problems	3.88	51.16
10	18.8	3.7.D	May not know appropriate units for mass	3.91	42.07, 42.08
11	18.4	3.7.A	May not understand how to locate points on a number line	3.82	35.15
12	18.2	3.7.C	May have difficulty solving problems that involve elapsed time	3.87	51.16
13	18.5	3.7.D	May not recognize a reasonable amount for capacity	3.89	43.07, 43.11
14	18.7	3.7.D, 3.7.E	May not know how many ounces are in one pound	3.90	42.05, 42.06
15	18.1	3.7.C	May not understand how to subtract intervals of time	3.86	51.16
16	18.5	3.7.D	May not recognize a reasonable amount for capacity	3.89	43.07, 43.11
17	18.4	3.7.A	May not understand how to convert fractions on a number line	3.82	35.15
18	18.8	3.7.E	May not understand the balance	3.91	42.07, 42.08
19	18.2	3.7.C	May not understand how to subtract intervals of time	3.87	51.16
20	18.6	3.7.E	May not recognize a reasonable amount for liquid volume	3.92	43.9, 43.10

*TEKS—Texas Essential Knowledge and Skills; **RtI**—Response to Intervention

Unit 4 Test

Item	Lesson	TEKS*	Common Error	Intervene with RtI* Tier 1 Lessons	Soar to Success Math
1	18.6	3.7.D	May not know appropriate units for liquid volume	3.92	43.09, 43.10
2	17.3	3.7.B	May not understand how to find the length of the missing side	3.85	47.31
3	18.2	3.7.C	May have difficulty solving problems that involve elapsed time	3.87	51.16
4	16.4	3.6.E	May not understand that equal parts can be different shapes	3.81	5.10
5	17.1	3.7.B	May miscount the units	3.83	47.30
6	15.2	3.6.B	May not know the names and attributes of quadrilaterals	3.75	38.31
7	16.1	3.6.D	May find the perimeter instead of area	3.79	48.31
8	18.4	3.7.A	May not understand how to locate points on a number line	3.82	35.15
9	18.8	3.7.E	May not understand how to use a balance	3.91	42.07, 42.08
10	16.3	3.6.C	May not understand how area changes with changes in length or width	3.77	48.28
11	17.2	3.7.B	May not measure correctly	3.84	47.30
12	18.1	3.7.C	May have difficulty subtracting intervals of time	3.86	51.16
13	16.2	3.6.C	May miscount the number of rows and columns	3.76	48.28
14	15.4	3.6.E	May not understand congruence	3.80	38.17, 40.17
15	15.1	3.6.B	May not correctly identify plane shapes	3.72	38.31

*TEKS—Texas Essential Knowledge and Skills; **RtI**—Response to Intervention

Unit 4 Test (continued)

Item	Lesson	TEKS*	Common Error	Intervene with RtI* Tier 1 Lessons	Soar to Success Math
16	18.5	3.7.D	May not understand units of capacity	3.89	43.07, 43.11
17	15.3	3.6.B	May not understand attributes of quadrilaterals.	3.73	38.31
18	17.1	3.7.B	May only add the lengths of two sides	3.83	47.30
19	16.5	3.6.C	May not count squares correctly	3.78	43.29
20	18.7	3.7.D	May not know how many ounces are in one pound	3.90	42.05, 42.06
21	15.5	3.6.A	May not correctly name three-dimensional solids	3.74	39.28, 39.29, 39.30, 39.33
22	16.5	3.6.D	May not decompose figure correctly	48.29	3.78
23	18.2	3.7.C	May have difficulty solving problems that involve elapsed time	3.87	51.16
24	18.4	3.7.A	May not understand how to locate points on a number line	3.82	35.15
25	16.4	3.6.E	May not understand unit fractions	3.81	5.10
26	15.1	3.6.A	May not understand characteristics of a rectangle	3.72	38.31
27	15.2	3.6.B	May not correctly identify plane shapes	3.75	38.31
28	18.5	3.7.D	May not understand how to convert from larger to smaller units of capacity	3.89	43.07, 43.11
29	18.6	3.7.E	May not recognize a reasonable amount for liquid volume	3.92	43.09, 43.10
30	17.3	3.7.B	May not understand how to find the length of the missing side	3.85	47.31

*TEKS—Texas Essential Knowledge and Skills; **RtI**—Response to Intervention

Unit 5 Test

Item	Lesson	TEKS*	Common Error	Intervene with RtI* Tier 1 Lessons	Soar to Success Math
1	19.2	3.8.B 3.8.A	May not understand how to read the pictograph	3.94	54.12, 54.14
2	19.2	3.8.B 3.8.A	May not understand how to read the pictograph	3.94	54.12, 54.14
3	19.5	3.8.B 3.8.A	May interpret the dot plot incorrectly	3.97	54.17
4	19.5	3.8.B 3.8.A	May interpret the dot plot incorrectly	3.97	54.17
5	19.5	3.8.B 3.8.A	May interpret the dot plot incorrectly	3.97	54.17
6	19.1	3.8.B 3.8.A	May have difficulty solving multi-step problems	3.93	54.03
7	19.1	3.8.B 3.8.A	May have difficulty reading the frequency table	3.93	54.03
8	19.2	3.8.B 3.8.A	May not read the pictograph correctly	3.94	54.12, 54.14
9	19.2	3.8.B 3.8.A	May not read the pictograph correctly	3.94	54.12, 54.14
10	19.3 19.4	3.8.B 3.8.A	May not read the bar graph correctly	3.95 3.96	54.13, 54.15 54.16
11	19.3 19.4	3.8.B 3.8.A	May have difficulty solving multi-step problems	3.95 3.96	54.13, 54.15 54.16
12	19.5	3.8.B 3.8.A	May have difficulty solving multi-step problems	3.94	54.12, 54.14
13	19.5	3.8.B 3.8.A	May have difficulty reading the dot plot	3.94	54.12, 54.14
14	19.3 19.4	3.8.B 3.8.A	May not read the bar graph correctly	3.95 3.96	54.13, 54.15 54.16
15	19.3 19.4	3.8.B 3.8.A	May not read the bar graph correctly	3.95 3.96	54.13, 54.15 54.16

*TEKS—Texas Essential Knowledge and Skills; **RtI**—Response to Intervention

Unit 5 Test (continued)

Item	Lesson	TEKS*	Common Error	Intervene with RtI* Tier 1 Lessons	Soar to Success Math
16	19.5	3.8.B 3.8.A	May not read the dot plot correctly	3.94	54.12, 54.14
17	19.5	3.8.B 3.8.A	May not understand how to display data on a dot plot	3.94	54.12, 54.14
18	19.3 19.4	3.8.B 3.8.A	May not read the bar graph correctly	3.95 3.96	54.13, 54.15 54.16
19	19.3 19.4	3.8.B 3.8.A	May have difficulty solving multi-step problems	3.95 3.96	54.13, 54.15 54.16
20	19.1	3.8.B 3.8.A	May have difficulty solving multi-step problems	3.93	54.03
21	19.1	3.8.B 3.8.A	May not read the frequency table correctly	3.93	54.03
22	19.1	3.8.B 3.8.A	May not understand how to read the frequency table	3.93	54.03
23	19.1	3.8.B 3.8.A	May have difficulty solving multi-step problems	3.93	54.03
24	19.2	3.8.B 3.8.A	May not understand how to use the key to read the pictograph	3.94	54.12, 54.14
25	19.2	3.8.B 3.8.A	May not understand how to use the key to read the pictograph	3.94	54.12, 54.14

*TEKS—Texas Essential Knowledge and Skills; **RtI**—Response to Intervention

Unit 6 Test

Item	Lesson	TEKS*	Common Error	Intervene with RtI* Tier 1 Lessons	Soar to Success Math
1	20.3	3.9.C	May not understand unplanned spending	3.61	61.02
2	20.5	3.9.E	May not read the table correctly	3.71	33.15, 33.16
3	20.6	3.9.F	May not understand saving	3.21	70.02
4	20.1	3.9.A	May subtract instead of dividing	3.39	12.49
5	20.4	3.9.D	May not complete both parts of the problem	3.64	71.03
6	20.1	3.9.A	May add instead of multiplying	3.39	12.49
7	20.6	3.9.F	May not understand giving	3.21	70.02
8	20.6	3.9.F	May not understand income	3.21	70.02
9	20.3	3.9.C	May not complete both parts of the problem	3.61	61.02
10	20.5	3.9.E	May not understand savings plans	3.71	33.15, 33.16
11	20.6	3.9.F	May not understand income	3.21	70.02
12	20.5	3.9.E	May multiply incorrectly	3.71	33.15, 33.16
13	20.4	3.9.D	May not understand credit	3.64	71.03
14	20.2	3.9.B	May not understand how scarcity affects price	3.5	7.32, 7.33
15	20.5	3.9.E	May not understand reasons for saving	3.71	33.15, 33.16
16	20.3	3.9.C	May not understand saving and spending	3.61	61.02

*TEKS—Texas Essential Knowledge and Skills; **RtI**—Response to Intervention

Unit 6 Test (continued)

Item	Lesson	TEKS*	Common Error	Intervene with RtI* Tier 1 Lessons	Soar to Success Math
17	20.6	3.9.F	May not understand credit	3.21	70.02
18	20.3	3.9.C	May not complete both parts of the problem	3.61	61.02
19	20.4	3.9.D	May not complete both parts of the problem	3.64	71.03
20	20.2	3.9.B	May not understand how scarcity affects price	3.5	7.32, 7.33
21	20.6	3.9.F	May not understand spending	3.21	70.02
22	20.3	3.9.C	May add instead of subtract	3.61	61.02
23	20.3	3.9.C	May not complete both parts of the problem	3.61	61.02
24	20.6	3.9.F	May not understand giving	3.21	70.02
25	20.4	3.9.D	May not complete both parts of the problem	3.64	71.03
26	20.2	3.9.B	May not understand how scarcity relates to price	3.5	7.32, 7.33
27	20.6	3.9.F	May not understand credit	3.21	70.02
28	20.5	3.9.E	May add instead of multiply	3.71	33.15, 33.16
29	20.6	3.9.F	May not understand saving	3.21	70.02
30	20.3	3.9.C	May not complete both parts of the problem	3.61	61.02

*TEKS—Texas Essential Knowledge and Skills; **RtI**—Response to Intervention

Correlations

Texas Essential Knowledge and Skills for Mathematics		Test: Item Numbers
3.2	**Number and operations.** The student applies mathematical process standards to represent and compare whole numbers and understand relationships related to place value. The student is expected to:	
3.2.A	compose and decompose numbers to 100,000 as a sum of so many ten thousands, so many thousands, so many hundreds, so many tens, and so many ones using objects, pictorial models, and numbers, including expanded notation as appropriate;	Module 1 Test: 1, 2, 3, 9, 10, 16, 17, 20 Unit 1 Test: 14, 22, 30 Beginning-/Middle-/End-of-Year Tests: 6
3.2.B	describe the mathematical relationships found in the base-10 place value system through the hundred thousands place;	Module 1 Test: 4, 8, 12 Unit 1 Test: 8 Beginning-/Middle-/End-of-Year Tests: 28
3.2.C	represent a number on a number line as being between two consecutive multiples of 10; 100; 1,000; or 10,000 and use words to describe relative size of numbers in order to round whole numbers; and	Module 1 Test: 5, 11, 13, 14, 15 Unit 1 Test: 17 Beginning-/Middle-/End-of-Year Tests: 41
3.2.D	compare and order whole numbers up to 100,000 and represent comparisons using the symbols >, <, or =.	Module 1 Test: 6, 7, 18, 19 Unit 1 Test: 4, 29 Beginning-/Middle-/End-of-Year Tests: 33, 42
3.3	**Number and operations.** The student applies mathematical process standards to represent and explain fractional units. The student is expected to:	
3.3.A	represent fractions greater than zero and less than or equal to one with denominators of 2, 3, 4, 6, and 8 using concrete objects and pictorial models, including strip diagrams and number lines;	Module 2 Test: 1, 2, 6, 8, 11, 12, 13, 14, 17, 19 Module 3 Test: 3, 12 Unit 1 Test: 16, 23 Beginning-/Middle-/End-of-Year Tests: 4
3.3.B	determine the corresponding fraction greater than zero and less than or equal to one with denominators of 2, 3, 4, 6, and 8 given a specified point on a number line;	Module 2 Test: 3, 16, 20 Module 3 Test: 13, 20 Beginning-/Middle-/End-of-Year Tests: 46
3.3.C	explain that the unit fraction $1/b$ represents the quantity formed by one part of a whole that has been partitioned into b equal parts where b is a non-zero whole number;	Module 2 Test: 10 Unit 1 Test: 18 Beginning-/Middle-/End-of-Year Tests: 26
3.3.D	compose and decompose a fraction a/b with a numerator greater than zero and less than or equal to b as a sum of parts $1/b$;	Module 2 Test: 4, 5 Unit 1 Test: 1 Beginning-/Middle-/End-of-Year Tests: 11
3.3.E	solve problems involving partitioning an object or a set of objects among two or more recipients using pictorial representations of fractions with denominators of 2, 3, 4, 6, and 8	Module 2 Test: 7, 9, 15, 18 Module 3 Test: 15 Unit 1 Test: 6 Beginning-/Middle-/End-of-Year Tests: 36
3.3.F	represent equivalent fractions with denominators of 2, 3, 4, 6, and 8 using a variety of objects and pictorial models, including number lines;	Module 3 Test: 5, 7, 9, 10, 11, 17, 18 Unit 1 Test: 10, 26 Beginning-/Middle-/End-of-Year Tests: 31
3.3.G	explain that two fractions are equivalent if and only if they are both represented by the same point on the number line or represent the same portion of a same size whole for an area model; and	Module 3 Test: 1 Unit 1 Test: 24 Beginning-/Middle-/End-of-Year Tests: 34

Correlations

	Texas Essential Knowledge and Skills for Mathematics	Test: Item Numbers
3.3.H	compare two fractions having the same numerator or denominator in problems by reasoning about their sizes and justifying the conclusion using symbols, words, objects, and pictorial models	Module 3 Test: 2, 4, 6, 8, 14, 16, 19 Unit 1 Test: 5, 20, 28 Beginning-/Middle-/End-of-Year Tests: 30
3.4	**Number and operations.** The student applies mathematical process standards to develop and use strategies and methods for whole number computations in order to solve problems with efficiency and accuracy. The student is expected to:	
3.4.A	solve with fluency one-step and two-step problems involving addition and subtraction within 1,000 using strategies based on place value, properties of operations, and the relationship between addition and subtraction;	Module 4 Test: 4, 6, 7, 8, 10, 13, 14, 15, 18, 19, 20 Module 5 Test: 1, 2, 3, 6, 7, 8, 10, 11, 12, 14, 15, 16, 18, 20 Unit 1 Test: 3, 9, 13, 15, 25 Beginning-/Middle-/End-of-Year Tests: 20, 37
3.4.B	round to the nearest 10 or 100 or use compatible numbers to estimate solutions to addition and subtraction problems;	Module 4 Test: 1, 3, 5, 9, 11, 12, 17 Module 5 Test: 4, 5, 9, 13, 17, 19 Unit 1 Test: 7, 11, 19, 21, 27 Beginning-/Middle-/End-of-Year Tests: 35
3.4.C	determine the value of a collection of coins and bills;	Module 4 Test: 2, 16 Unit 1 Test: 2 Beginning-/Middle-/End-of-Year Tests: 17
3.4.D	determine the total number of objects when equally-sized groups of objects are combined or arranged in arrays up to 10 by 10;	Module 6 Test: 15, 16, 20 Unit 2 Test: 26, 30 Beginning-/Middle-/End-of-Year Tests: 22
3.4.E	represent multiplication facts by using a variety of approaches such as repeated addition, equal-sized groups, arrays, area models, equal jumps on a number line, and skip counting;	Module 6 Test: 3, 5, 7, 9, 11, 13 Module 7 Test: 3, 4, 6, 7, 13, 14, 19 Module 8 Test: 1, 5, 7, 15, 16, 20 Module 9 Test: 1, 12 Unit 2 Test: 5, 9, 12, 13, 21 Beginning-/Middle-/End-of-Year Tests: 21
3.4.F	recall facts to multiply up to 10 by 10 with automaticity and recall the corresponding division facts;	Module 8 Test: 2, 8, 18 Module 11 Test: 3, 11, 16 Module 12 Test: 3, 18 Unit 2 Test: 2, 22 Beginning-/Middle-/End-of-Year Tests: 39
3.4.G	use strategies and algorithms, including the standard algorithm, to multiply a two-digit number by a one-digit number. Strategies may include mental math, partial products, and the commutative, associative, and distributive properties;	Module 9 Test: 2, 3, 4, 5, 6, 8, 9, 11, 14, 15, 17, 18, 20 Unit 2 Test: 8, 18, 24, 27 Beginning-/Middle-/End-of-Year Tests: 9
3.4.H	determine the number of objects in each group when a set of objects is partitioned into equal shares or a set of objects is shared equally;	Module 10 Test: 2, 9, 12, 13, 18, 20 Module 11 Test: 1, 5, 12, 14 Module 12 Test: 7, 11 Module 13 Test: 1, 5, 13, 19 Unit 2 Test: 3, 16 Beginning-/Middle-/End-of-Year Tests: 27

Correlations

	Texas Essential Knowledge and Skills for Mathematics	Test: Item Numbers
3.4.I	determine if a number is even or odd using divisibility rules;	Module 11 Test: 2, 4, 8, 10, 13, 17, 19 Unit 2 Test: 6, 15 Beginning-/Middle-/End-of-Year Tests: 7
3.4.J	determine a quotient using the relationship between multiplication and division; and	Module 11 Test: 6, 15, 20 Module 12 Test: 8 Module 13 Test: 2, 10, 17 Unit 2 Test: 7 Beginning-/Middle-/End-of-Year Tests: 1
3.4.K	solve one-step and two-step problems involving multiplication and division within 100 using strategies based on objects; pictorial models including arrays, area models, and equal groups; properties of operations; or recall of facts.	Module 6 Test: 1, 2, 4, 6, 8, 10, 12, 14, 17, 18, 19 Module 7 Test: 1, 2, 5, 8, 9, 10, 11, 12, 15, 16, 17, 18, 20 Module 8 Test: 3, 4, 6, 9, 10, 11, 12, 13, 14, 17, 19 Module 9 Test: 7, 10, 13, 16, 19 Module 10 Test: 1, 3, 4, 5, 6, 7, 8, 10, 11, 14, 15, 16, 17, 19 Module 11 Test: 7, 9, 18 Module 12 Test: 1, 2, 4, 5, 6, 9, 10, 12, 13, 14, 15, 16, 17, 19, 20 Module 13 Test: 3, 4, 6, 7, 8, 9, 11, 12, 14, 15, 16, 18, 20 Unit 2 Test: 1, 4, 10, 11, 14, 17, 19, 20, 23, 25, 28, 29 Beginning-/Middle-/End-of-Year Tests: 16, 45
3.5	**Algebraic reasoning.** The student applies mathematical process standards to analyze and create patterns and relationships. The student is expected to:	Unit 3 Test: 21
3.5.A	represent one- and two-step problems involving addition and subtraction of whole numbers to 1,000 using pictorial models, number lines, and equations;	Unit 3 Test: 2, 6, 8, 12, 14, 17, 23, 24, 29, 30 Beginning-/Middle-/End-of-Year Tests: 14
3.5.B	represent and solve one- and two-step multiplication and division problems within 100 using arrays, strip diagrams, and equations;	Unit 3 Test: 1, 7, 9, 10, 11, 16, 18, 20, 25, 26, 27, 28 Beginning-/Middle-/End-of-Year Tests: 32
3.5.C	describe a multiplication expression as a comparison such as 3×24 represents 3 times as much as 24;	Unit 3 Test: 5 Beginning-/Middle-/End-of-Year Tests: 38
3.5.D	determine the unknown whole number in a multiplication or division equation relating three whole numbers when the unknown is either a missing factor or product; and	Unit 3 Test: 3, 13, 19, 22 Beginning-/Middle-/End-of-Year Tests: 15, 25
3.5.E	represent real-world relationships using number pairs in a table and verbal descriptions.	Unit 3 Test: 4, 15 Beginning-/Middle-/End-of-Year Tests: 29
3.6	**Geometry and measurement.** The student applies mathematical process standards to analyze attributes of two-dimensional geometric figures to develop generalizations about their properties. The student is expected to:	

Correlations

	Texas Essential Knowledge and Skills for Mathematics	Test: Item Numbers
3.6.A	classify and sort two- and three-dimensional solids, including cones, cylinders, spheres, triangular and rectangular prisms, and cubes, based on attributes using formal geometric language;	Module 15 Test: 2, 4, 5, 9, 11, 13, 17, 18, 19, 20 Unit 4 Test: 21, 26 Beginning-/Middle-/End-of-Year Tests: 40
3.6.B	use attributes to recognize rhombuses, parallelograms, trapezoids, rectangles, and squares as examples of quadrilaterals and draw examples of quadrilaterals that do not belong to any of these subcategories;	Module 15 Test: 1, 3, 7, 8, 10, 12, 15, 16 Unit 4 Test: 6, 15, 17, 27 Beginning-/Middle-/End-of-Year Tests: 44
3.6.C	determine the area of rectangles with whole number side lengths in problems using multiplication related to the number of rows times the number of unit squares in each row;	Module 16 Test: 1, 5, 10, 11, 15 Unit 4 Test: 10, 13, 19 Beginning-/Middle-/End-of-Year Tests: 2
3.6.D	decompose composite figures formed by rectangles into non-overlapping rectangles to determine the area of the original figure using the additive property of area; and	Module 16 Test: 2, 4, 8, 13, 16 Unit 4 Test: 7, 22 Beginning-/Middle-/End-of-Year Tests: 19
3.6.E	decompose two congruent two-dimensional figures into parts with equal areas and express the area of each part as a unit fraction of the whole and recognize that equal shares of identical wholes need not have the same shape.	Module 15 Test: 6, 14 Module 16 Test: 3, 6, 7, 9, 12, 14 Unit 4 Test: 4, 14, 25 Beginning-/Middle-/End-of-Year Tests: 24
3.7	**Geometry and measurement.** The student applies mathematical process standards to select appropriate units, strategies, and tools to solve problems involving customary and metric measurement. The student is expected to:	
3.7.A	represent fractions of halves, fourths, and eighths as distances from zero on a number line;	Module 18 Test: 4, 11, 17 Unit 4 Test: 8, 24 Beginning-/Middle-/End-of-Year Tests: 8
3.7.B	determine the perimeter of a polygon or a missing length when given perimeter and remaining side lengths in problems;	Module 17 Test: 1–19 Unit 4 Test: 2, 5, 11, 18, 30 Beginning-/Middle-/End-of-Year Tests: 3
3.7.C	determine the solutions to problems involving addition and subtraction of time intervals in minutes using pictorial models or tools such as a 15-minute event plus a 30-minute event equals 45 minutes;	Module 18 Test: 1, 3, 5, 8, 9, 12, 15, 19 Unit 4 Test: 3, 12, 23 Beginning-/Middle-/End-of-Year Tests: 10
3.7.D	determine when it is appropriate to use measurements of liquid volume (capacity) or weight; and	Module 18 Test: 2, 6, 7, 10, 13, 14, 16 Unit 4 Test: 1, 16, 20, 28 Beginning-/Middle-/End-of-Year Tests: 18
3.7.E	determine liquid volume (capacity) or weight using appropriate units and tools.	Module 18 Test: 2, 6, 7, 14, 18, 20 Unit 4 Test: 9, 29 Beginning-/Middle-/End-of-Year Tests: 23
3.8	**Data analysis.** The student applies mathematical process standards to solve problems by collecting, organizing, displaying, and interpreting data. The student is expected to:	

Correlations

	Texas Essential Knowledge and Skills for Mathematics	Test: Item Numbers
3.8.A	summarize a data set with multiple categories using a frequency table, dot plot, pictograph, or bar graph with scaled intervals; and	Unit 5 Test: 1–25 Beginning-/Middle-/End-of-Year Tests: 50
3.8.B	solve one- and two-step problems using categorical data represented with a frequency table, dot plot, pictograph, or bar graph with scaled intervals.	Unit 5 Test: 1–25 Beginning-/Middle-/End-of-Year Tests: 49
3.9	**Personal financial literacy.** The student applies mathematical process standards to manage one's financial resources effectively for lifetime financial security. The student is expected to:	
3.9.A	explain the connection between human capital/labor and income;	Unit 6 Test: 4, 6 Beginning-/Middle-/End-of-Year Tests: 5
3.9.B	describe the relationship between the availability or scarcity of resources and how that impacts cost;	Unit 6 Test: 14, 20, 26 Beginning-/Middle-/End-of-Year Tests: 48
3.9.C	identify the costs and benefits of planned and unplanned spending decisions;	Unit 6 Test: 1, 9, 16, 18, 22, 23, 30 Beginning-/Middle-/End-of-Year Tests: 47
3.9.D	explain that credit is used when wants or needs exceed the ability to pay and that it is the borrower's responsibility to pay it back to the lender, usually with interest;	Unit 6 Test: 5, 13, 19, 25 Beginning-/Middle-/End-of-Year Tests: 13
3.9.E	list reasons to save and explain the benefit of a savings plan, including for college; and	Unit 6 Test: 2, 10, 12, 15, 28 Beginning-/Middle-/End-of-Year Tests: 12
3.9.F	identify decisions involving income, spending, saving, credit, and charitable giving.	Unit 6 Test: 3, 7, 8, 11, 17, 21, 24, 27, 29 Beginning-/Middle-/End-of-Year Tests: 43